USERS AND USES OF LIBRARY

USERS AND USES OF LIBRARY

Dr. P. BALASUBRAMANIAN
M.A., M.L.I.Sc., M.Phil., PGDCA, PGDPR, Ph.D.
Deputy Librarian
Manonmaniam Sundaranar University
Tirunelveli (T.N.)

DEEP & DEEP PUBLICATIONS PVT. LTD.
F-159, Rajouri Garden, New Delhi - 110 027

USERS AND USES OF LIBRARY

ISBN 978-81-8450-300-5

Typeset by RAHUL COMPOSERS
358, Pocket-B, Phase-2, Sector-16B, Dwarka, New Delhi - 110 075

Printed in India at MAYUR ENTERPRISES
WZ Plot No. 3, Gujjar Market, Tihar Village, New Delhi - 110 018

Published by DEEP & DEEP PUBLICATIONS PVT. LTD.,
F-159, Rajouri Garden, New Delhi - 110 027 • Phone : 25435369, 25440916
E-mail : ddpubs@gmail.com • ddpbooks@yahoo.co.in
Showroom :
2/13, Ansari Road, Daryaganj, New Delhi - 110 002 • Telefax : 23245122

Contents

Preface

This book has been written on "Library Uses and Users Research" to meet the requirements of the students of B.L.I.Sc., M.L.I.Sc., M.Phil. and Ph.D. in Library and Information Science professional courses.

Every article is written exhaustively giving elaborate information.

I am greatly indebted to Deep & Deep Publications Pvt. Ltd., New Delhi, the most popular and leading publisher of books. In a short period, they have taken the utmost care, skill and interest in bringing this book.

Any comments and suggestions for the improvement of this book will be gratefully acknowledged and incorporated in the next edition.

DR. P. BALASUBRAMANIAN

Acknowledgements

The authors feels extremely indebted to Dr. R.T. Sabapathi Mohan, Vice-Chancellor, Manonmaniam Sundaranar University, Tirunelveli and all the teaching and non-teaching staff members of the M.S. University for giving me constant encouragement for writing this book.

I also thank Prof. Dr. A. Rangaswamy, Professor, Management Studies, Infant Jesus College of Engineering, Thoothukudi for help and suggestions.

I would like to thank my beloved wife **Mrs. B. Devi** and my children who shared my burden and helped me in many ways during the preparation of this book.

I would be a benefit killer if I do not acknowledge the services of Deep & Deep Publications Pvt. Ltd., New Delhi for their efforts in bringing out this book in a record time. Suggestions for further improvement of the book are most welcome.

DR. P. BALASUBRAMANIAN

1

A Study on the Library Utilization

INTRODUCTION

Information is the very basis of human existence. It is undoubtedly and increasing be recognized that information is a vital resource. Information is an indispensable raw material for right decision-making from the governmental and institutional level to the personal level. It is in fact a vital ingredient for the social development of any nation especially developing countries like India. It is a well accepted generalization that a country which is rich in information is rich in the social-economic spheres.

As it is an age of knowledge and information revolution, necessity is there to make a useful practical distinction by defining knowledge and information. Information is the essential element for this progress of higher education. There are terms of information such as knowledge, facts, data, news, message, etc. The implicit assumption of user studies, behaviour studies and information flow studies is that if one understands user needs and problems, one can design effective information systems.

The word 'in' is used, in the content of user studies research, to denote a physical entity of phenomenon (as information the case of questions relating to the number of books read on information in a period of time, the number of journals subscribed to, etc.) the channel of communication through which messages are transferred as and when we speek of the incidence of oral *versus* written information), or the factual data, empirically determined and presented information as a document or transmitted orally.

Within the field of user studies the investigation of 'information' needs has presented seemingly intractable problems. If we date user studies from 1984 and the Royal Society Scientific Information Conference, with its several surveys of user's information access pattern then the progress towards some theoretical understanding of the concept of information needs has been slow.

This fact is recognized by virtually every commentator on the subject from Menzel and Paisley through the various authors' information the ARIST Volumes to Ford's review of 1977. As well as flawing attention to this fact, the authors have tried to discover why it is so and have generally concluded that the reason lies information adequate methodology and the failure to do research that is cumulative. Attention has also been paid to the definite problem of information need.

However, many (if not most) information scientists are practitioners in information work or information systems management, and they look at studies of information needs for guidance on aspects of systems doing, development and operation. A confusion then arises between what is intended by information needs research and what is expected of such research. There is another confusion, possibly more basic, information the association of the two words information and needs. This association imbues the resulting concept with connotations of a basic need qualitatively similar to other basic human needs. However, if we examine the literature on human needs we find that this concept is divided by psychologists into three categories.

- Physiological needs, such as the need for food, water, shelter, etc.
- Affective needs, such as the need for attainment, for domination, etc.
- Cognitive needs, such as the need to plan, to learn a skill, etc.

One of the important land marks in the history of user studies was the establishment of the centre for research on user studies information 1975 at the University of Sheffield. The centre became fully operational on 1st January 1976.

Information access patterns of the group will assist the library more effectively in developing programmes and using resources and limited funds to desired goals. Accurate and up-to-date knowledge about user and their information patterns are the essential ingredients in the library system.

Information

Information means the communication of knowledge about an event of a given condition or the spread of knowledge derived from observation, study, experience or instruction. According to Bhattacharyya (1978) Information is the message conveyed or intended to be conveyed by a systemizing body of ideas, or its accepted or acceptable substitutes. Information has become an essential commodity for the man to perform his social value. It is vital to the proper functioning of a democratic society, a crucial tool information an economy and an effective government, a central part of the growth and well-being of individuals.

Definition

Kent (1979) states that Information is the feed stock for knowledge. Information an idea would be unimpeded flow of information amongst individuals of equal capacity to process the information into knowledge there would be no advantage to be gained by any individual or group as compared with another by possession of information. Davis (1974) has defined information as data that has been processed into a form that is meaningful to the recipient and of real perceived value information current or perspective decision.

Further, Buckland (1991) distinguishes three meanings of information by analyzing the dictionary meanings given in the Oxford English Dictionary, 1989—

1. *Information-as-process* : when some one is informed, what they know is changed. In this change "information" is "the act of information; communication of the knowledge or new of some fact or occurrence; the action of telling or fact of being told of something".
2. *Information-as-a knowledge* : "information is also used to denote that which is perceived in information-as-a process; the "knowledge communicated concerning some particular fact, subject or event; that of which one is appraised or told, intelligence, news".
3. *Information-as-a thing* : The term 'information' is also used attributively for objects, such as data and documents, that are referred to as 'information' because they are regarded as being information, as 'having the quality or imparting knowledge' or communicating information; instructive.

Putting together various definitions of the scientists it can be expressed that information is processed data of value; produced by any segments of the society. As and when more information is added to the existing knowledge structure, it gets modified. In other words, it can be said that information is the feed stock for knowledge. Information is flow of messages is piece-meal or fragment having the natural of timeliness and transitory.

Whereas in the Oxford English Dictionary, information is taken as a verb and the following meanings are given.

- Communication of instructive knowledge.
- Communication of knowledge or news of some fact or occurrence.
- Knowledge communicated concerning some particular fact, subject or event.

Kinds of Information

Koblitz (1969) distinguishers three kinds of information with which we can note the nature of information at various stages being used information of the society. The three kinds of information are:

- Semantic Information (as a message) is a unit composed of meaning and carrier for the purpose of transmission of knowledge and experience from one subject to another. Here, the information is having, the nature of a message. In this process, information has clear meaning and transmitted the knowledge and experience of one person to the other.
- Semantic Information (as a process) is of purposeful action for the creation (including handling), storage, searching and dissemination of information and coupled with sensory perception (infer reflection) or exchange of information between humans (bilateral).
- Documental information which contains new facts or statements of analytical or synthetic character. The nature of documental information is of facts or statements which have analysis or synthetic character. And these facts and statements are supported by evidences. Koblitz also called it factographic information.

User Study

User studies is a difficult area of knowledge to define. If can include conventional surveys of library borrowers and this may be the main form of activity which comes to mind when the term user studies-mentioned.

A user study may be defined as a systematic study of information requirements of users in order to facilitate meaningful exchanges between information system and users.

User studies are being conducted on the behaviour of the user information seeking information, instead of the needs of the user. These studies are more useful to study the user, his psychology, the working conditions, the impact of his position in the society, etc. with this the user group is studied information a better way to modify the services and tools of the information system.

According to Wysoki, user studies or use studies could be concerned with studying information processing activities of the users.

According the Cronin, user study is a willingness to relate product or system design to the perceived needs of those for whom the product or system is intended.

In the light of the above definition a study which is focused on user to understand directly or indirectly their information needs, use behaviour and access pattern I usually called user study.

Classification of User Studies

There are number of classification available on user studies. The user studies have been classified into different ways.

Menzel's Classification

In Menzel classification the user studies are broadly divided into three groups—

1. Behaviour studies
2. Use studies
3. Information flow studies

In the above said studies, which are carried out to know the pattern of overall interaction of their user community with the communication systems, without reference to any specific information receiving are called behaviour studies.

The studies which are conducted to find out the use of any communication medium such as primary periodical, other sources are called use studies.

The studies which are conducted to find the pattern of flow of information in the communication system are known as the information flow studies.

Cronin's Classification

According to Cronin, "The user studies may be either descriptive or perspective.

A descriptive study describes how information transfer that takes place information relation to a particular user population.

The perspective study will suggest ways in which the prevailing system or product could be modified or upgraded to ensure a greater degree of satisfaction.

Methods of User Study

Guha has categorized user study into a number of methods as the following:

1. General or conventional methods
2. Indirect method
3. Special and unconventional methods

General or Conventional Methods

This includes survey methods like questionnaire, interview, diary, observation by self and operation research. Of these, questionnaire and interview methods are very popular among investigators engaged in user studies.

A questionnaire is a set of questions framed with a view to ascertain the user needs, access pattern and use behaviour. There are two types of questionnaire.

(i) Structured, and
(ii) Unstructured

The structured questionnaire is generally used for the survey conducted by the questionnaire method. The unstructured questionnaire is used as a tool to conduct structured interview.

A questionnaire may contain different types of questions. Questions can be categorized as factual, general, open, closed, mixed, etc. Interview is another popular method which can be used for data collection in user studies.

There are two types of interviews:

(i) Structured interview
(ii) Unstructured interview

The structured interview is conducted by using a pre-designed questionnaire. In the unstructured interview the investigator may not be using a pre-designed questionnaire. The data collection by this method is expensive and time consuming.

Diary method is that information which users under study are asked to keep a detailed record of particular information activities such as reading, information research, discussions, etc.

Observation methods of various information activities are taken as the data. In this case, operation research study selected users are observed at random during working hours of a library and the time spent on various information activities recorded. The above techniques are time consuming and full co-operation of the users are essential to execute the survey.

Indirect Method

Indirect methods include analysis of library records and citation analysis. On the basis of the materials used by the users, investigators can ascertain the users' requirements indirectly. For the analysis of library records important records such as circulation statistics, inter-library loan record, personal indexes used by the researchers, service demand slips in the reference section, data label slips, etc., can be used. An analysis of the above said records will provide a partial view of user needs or user's requirements.

Citation analysis is a popular indirect method that can be used as a technique for user study. Citations or reference provided by authors in their documents became the basis of citation analysis. The implicit assumption is that the cited documents which used by authors and this is an index to the nature of materials required by the users. When compared to other methods, citation analysis is generally treated as unbiased. However, it has a number of demerits such as:

- Citation analysis will give only a partial idea about the use of materials and, secondly, tertiary sources, formal and informal sources, etc. are not usually cited by authors.
- The possibility of their citing unused material.
- The possibility of self-citation by certain authors, etc.

Special and Unconventional Methods

Special and unconventional methods include computer feedback which make use of records obtained as by-products of a computer search. The wider use of computer in libraries can bring these techniques into an effective one information ascertaining users requirements. By unconventional methods the investigator tries to know the way information which scientists work, the bibliographical, autobiographical sources, etc.

REVIEW OF LITERATURE

There have been number of Literature published so-far emphasizing need of the information seeking behaviours.

Wilson has discussed in his study that information seeking behaviour results from the recognition of some need, perceived by the user.

Garg and Ashok Kumar report that most of the information scientists collect procedural information for a design or development of the project. Periodical are highly used to the sources of information gathering and the average number of primary periodicals are scanned by the scientists.

Kawatra conducted a study on research scholars of three Universities of Rajasthan to know the views of scholars on the adequacy of library resources, and services.

Dutt has found the detailed requirements of the specific information services can be identified only after through the user needs and present the information seeking behaviour of the community, the user surveys for assessment of user needs may be said to be indispensable for the effective and efficient utilization of information system and services.

Vital Rao has made a study on the information seeking behaviour of scientists at National Institute of Nutrition, Hyderabad by questionnaire method.

A study has been made by Herner on 450 medical scientists on the use of formal and informal channels of communication. Results show that the majority of medical scientists got the idea of new project through personal contacts discussions with their colleagues and the remaining got from their personal work.

A survey was undertaken by Jasmer Singh and Harsingh to assess the needs and expectations of users of Punjab University Library, candidate. The study was examined the adequacy of library collection. Satisfaction of user with regard to landing, reference and bibliographic services.

Ellis analysed the information seeking behaviour among social scientists then discussed the use of electronic communication through electronic data based and computer based information online search.

Panwer and Vyas insist that teachers are the communicators to the students, their demand increases for references books and text books for their own intellectual development and students also engage themselves in research, therefore, basic reference works of important subjects need special attention and consideration by library authority, faculty members and library staff.

Deshmukh by his study suggests that overall collection of all types of literature is not completely adequate. Efforts should be made to improve the collection, Emphasis should be given to reports and reference books.

Sethi has made a study on information seeking behaviour of social scientists. Results indicated that they did not differ in respect to how they seek their information in their choice of channels and sources of information. The seeking behaviour of social scientists in developing and developed countries tent to be different on account of differences in the social systems. Infrastructure for collection is the storage utilization of information.

Rolinson *et. al.*, conducted a study of percentage, whereas the latter adopted the Chi-square (X^2) techniques.

Geeth and Biswas reported in their study that as students are our largest single group of users we keep most of them on our door steps only.

Krishnan Kumar (1968) has conducted a survey concerning teachers and research scholars in the Department of Chemistry, University of Delhi. The important finding of this survey was quite a large percentage of research fellows do not use the library as much as they ought to. The majority of the researchers (71 percent) feel the need to improve their skills in the use of Science & Technology literature.

Ford, Geoffrey (1973) conducted a survey on user behaviour in University libraries, in his analysis of use studies, the important finding of this review of research in user behaviour is that it has yet to be demonstrated that the use of libraries has any definite influence on any thing else.

A survey was made by Mallaiah and Badami to know the opinions of research scholars of the services and facilities of Mangalore, University Library.

A survey made by Sudharani and Veeransaneyulu to know the opinion most of the faculty members stated that they are satisfied with the services and information for human development of Sri Padmavathi Mahila Viswavidyalayam Tirupathi (A.P.).

Satyanarayanan in his finding, reports that information is a powerful instrument in society and it is a large part in improving the quality of life for individuals. The library should become a source of information for decision-making and socio-economic developments. Each community requires library services tailored to individual needs. They support co-operation of the communication for their information needs.

The study carried out Awogbami on the faculty members of twenty four Nigerian Universities to discover their perceptions of library and to determine the nature and extent of their interaction with the library.

Prasad and Tripathi carried out a study based on a sample of 26 physical and social scientists. So the findings can be generalized. Although the findings provide significant insight into the similarity and difference in the information seeking behaviour of physical and social scientists in India.

Abifarin says that most of the students do not know how to use the library catalogue which is the key to holding of each library. The reason for this is, it is time consuming and in the end not useful. The need to organize in service training for library assistants to equip them with the challenges associated with their duties in order to be more useful to students.

Sasikala has conducted a study to know the information seeking behaviour of managers working in 20 industrial organization of Andhra Pradesh, using a questionnaire. Some difference are found in their information seeking behaviour among the senior, middle and junior managers.

A survey made by Sudharani and Veeranjaneyulu to know the opinion most of the faculty members stated that they are satisfied with the services and informations for human development of Sri Padmavathi Mahila Viswavidyalayam Tirupathi (A.P.).

RESEARCH DESIGN

For the successful conduction of any research study for drawing meaningful inferences, an appropriate methodology is indispensable. The main focus of this study is to analyse the utilization of library by students of Polytechnic College.

Needs for the Study

This study is confined to the information seeking behaviour of users of Government Polytechnic College, Tuticorin. The main aim of the study is to measure the success and failure of working system of library, reading habits and the variety of interest of the user in their fields such as general and subject oriented and also it will be a guide for the librarians to procure the required documents so as to the result brought out.

Objectives of the Study

The following are the major objectives of the present study:

1. To identify the frequency of visit to library by the users of the Govt. Polytechnic College library.
2. To identify the purpose for which users may visit the library.
3. To assess the level of satisfaction on services provided in the library for users.
4. To find out the order of preference of documents by users of the library.
5. To know the searching methods followed by the uses to find their relevant documents/books.
6. To identify the users' satisfaction about the infrastructure, working time, procedures of the library.

Hypothesis

Based on the above mentioned objective the following hypothesis have been formulated and tested in the present study.

There would be a significant variation among different type of users.

- Frequency of visit to library
- Purpose of visit to library
- Overall satisfaction of library collection

Limitation of the Study

The study is restricted to only students users of Govt. Polytechnic College Library, Tuticorin. Among the students of the Government Polytechnic only three branches, i.e. Civil, Mechanical and Electrical and Electronics are taken for this study.

Methodology

The study is mainly based on the primary data collected from the college library users though a well-designed questionnaire. Also secondary data has been collected from sources like Text books, reference books, National and International Journals and Magazines.

Development of the Questionnaire and Collection of Data

The data was collected by using empirical method of questionnaire. At first, a pilot study was conducted to test the feelings among the respondents in answering the questions. Then the well tested questionnaire was distributed personally to the Library users. Sufficient time was given to the respondents in furnishing the data information. At the time of collecting for the field questionnaire each respondent was requested to offer his comments and opinion on various concepts included in it. Their suggestions relating to the improvement of library services were also called for.

About 180 questionnaires were distributed to the users of library and received back. Among the 180, 60 respondents from Civil, 60 respondents from mechanical and 60 respondents from ECE. Only engineering students are taken for this study.

Statistical Techniques

To analyse the collected data, simple percentages and two-way analysis of variance were applied.

- First Chapter given introduction about library users' study and ISB.
- Second Chapter deals with review of literature.
- Third Chapter examine research design which include objective, hypothesis, methodology, application of statistical tools.

- Fourth Chapter given the profiles of Government Polytechnic and its library, Tuticorin.
- Fifth Chapter deals with the result and discussion of the related study.
- Sixth Chapter deals with findings and conclusion.
- The result shows that the library providing various library services in very effective ways.
- The result shows that majority of the students are very much satisfied with the arrangement of reading material in the library.
- The results shows that in library fulfils the users requirements and nearly 60% of the respondents express as excellent library service.
- The result also found that nearly 70% of respondents prefer text books and it is followed by reference collection.
- The result found that more than 95% of the students are satisfied with infrastructure, working time and procedure of the library.

Suggestions

Suggestion, opinions and recommendations expressed by the respondents are listed below:

- It is suggested that the library should be introduced the open access system for its users population.
- It is also suggested that internet and automated library services may be given to users of the library.

RESULTS AND DISCUSSION

The present study tries to bring to lime light the ISB of the beneficiaries of the Government Polytechnic College, Tuticorin. In this chapter an attempt is made to present the results of the analysis of the data collected from the college library users. A description of the characteristics of the respondents of library visit, collection of information problems faced by the respondents and users satisfaction of the library.

TABLE 1
Language-wise Borrowing Books from the Library

Sl. No.	*Users*	*Languages*			
		Tamil	*English*	*Others*	*Total*
1.	Civil	28	30	2	60
2.	Mechanical	25	28	7	60
3.	Electrical and Electronics	24	32	4	60
	Total	77	90	13	180

Source : Primary Data.

Table 1 shows the languagewise borrowing of books from the library, irrespective of respondents, 50% of the users borrowed English medium books, 42.78% of them borrowed Tamil Medium books and 7.22% of them borrowed other language books. Therefore, majority of the users borrowed English Medium Books.

TABLE 2
User Satisfaction about Library Service

Sl. No.	*Users*	*Overall Library Service*		
		Yes	*No*	*Total*
1.	Civil	48	12	60
2.	Mechanical	51	9	60
3.	Electrical and Electronics	53	7	60
	Total	152	28	180

Source : Computer from Primary Data.

FIG. 1

Language-wise Borrowing Books from the Library

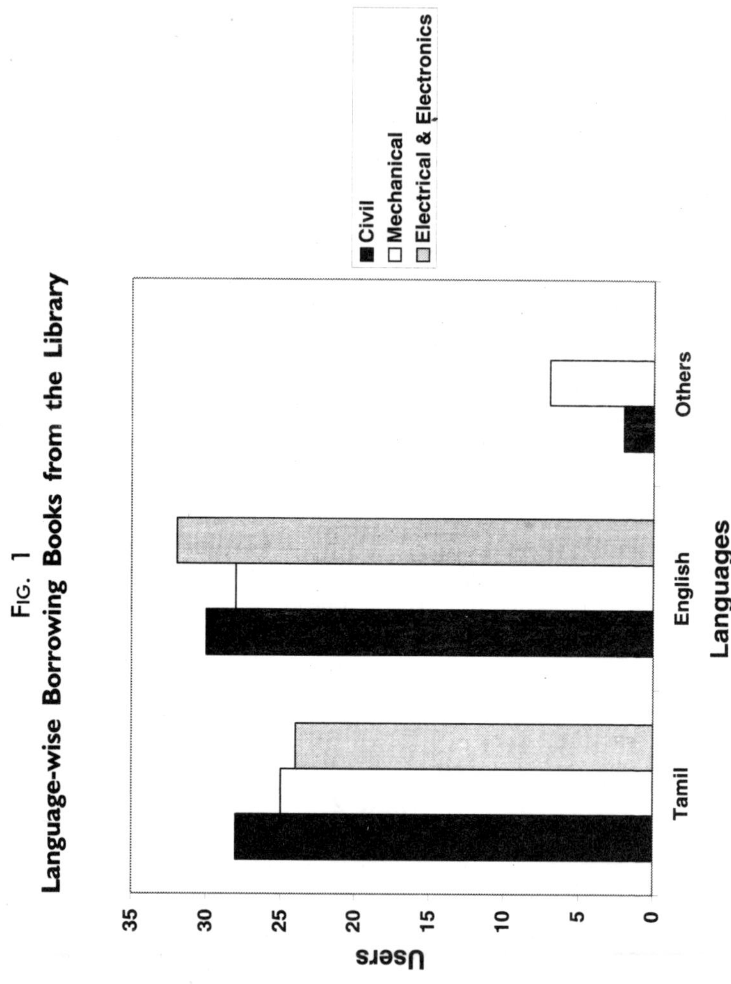

Fig. 2

User Satisfaction about Library Service

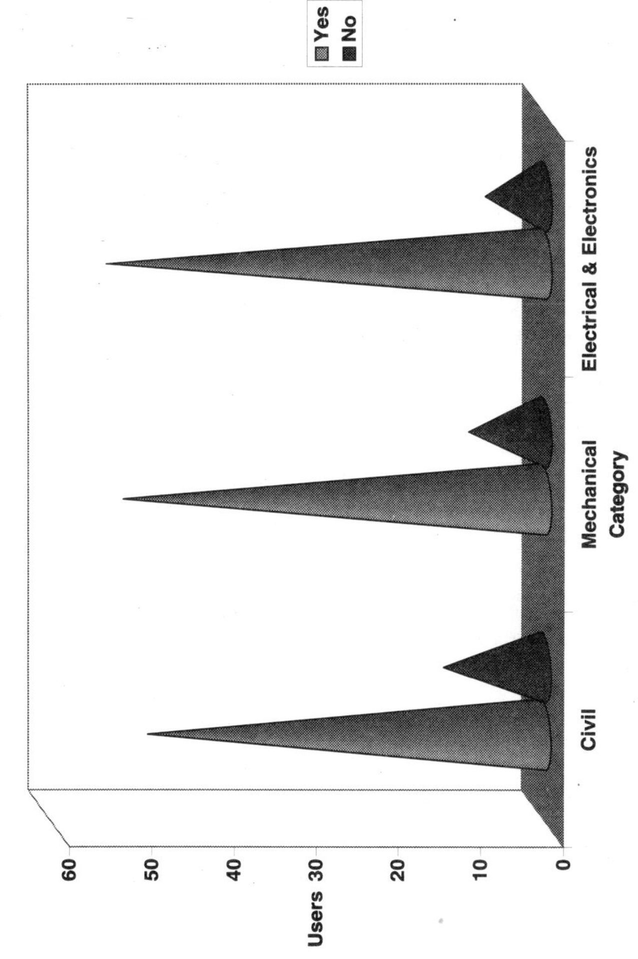

Table 2 shows the users satisfaction about overall library service, out of 180 respondents from three departments, irrespective of them, 84.44% of respondents satisfied with overall library service and only 15.56% of them are not satisfied with the library service.

TABLE 3
Frequency of Visit to the Library

Sl. No.	*Frequency & Visit Library*	*Civil*	*Mech.*	*E & E*	*Total*
1.	Daily	20	22	25	67
2.	Several Times/Week	18	17	18	53
3.	Once a Week	16	15	12	43
4.	Once a Month	06	04	03	13
5.	Occassionally	—	02	02	04
	Total	60	60	60	180

Source : Computer from Primary Data.

Table 3 shows the frequency of visit to the library, irrespective of the respondents 37.22% of them visit to library daily 29.44% of them visit to library daily, 27.44% of the visit to library several time per week, 23.89% once a week, 7.22% once a month, 2.22% occassionally.

FINDINGS AND SUGGESTIONS

- The sample population for this study is 180, and among them 60 (33.33%) Civil Branch students, 60 (33.33%) Mechanical students and 60 (33.33%) E & E branch students.
- Further the result found that majority of the users, i.e. males 126 (70%) and followed by females user 54 (30%).
- From the analysis of the frequency of the library visit by respondents it was found that more than

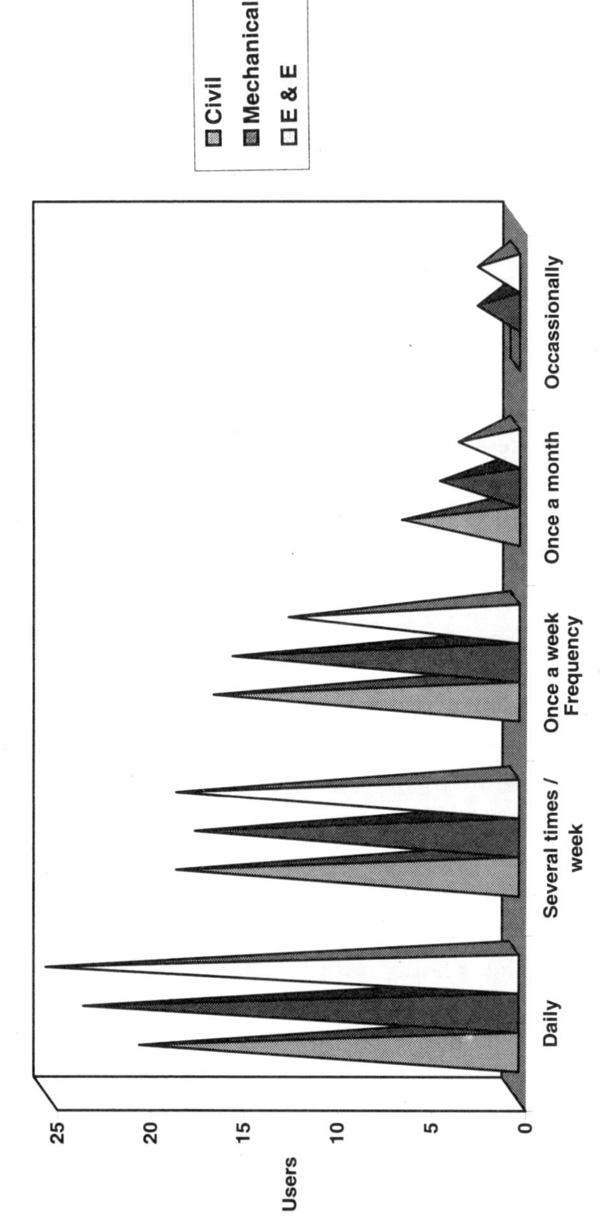

FIG. 3
Frequency of Visit to the Library

65% of the students visit the library daily and several times per week.

- The result also found that nearly 80% of the students spent up to one hour in the library.
- The result is reveals that English medium books are borrowed by student but at the same time more than 40% of the students used to borrow Tamil medium books also.
- It is also found from the result that more than 90% of students are satisfied with borrowing facilities.
- The result shows that majority of the users followed subject-wise approach.
- The result shows that nearly 90% of the students are satisfied with overall library collection.
- The results shows that nearly 85% of the students are satisfied with overall library service.
- The result shows that nearly 85% of the students agreed the rules and regulations of the library.
- The result shows that majority of the stuents are very much satisfied with the arrangement of reading material in the library.
- The results shows that in library fulfils the users requirements and nearly 60% of the respondents express as excellent library service.
- The result also found that nearly 70% of respondents prefer text books and it is followed by reference collection.
- The result found that more than 95% of the students are satisfied with infrastructure, working time and procedure of the library.

Suggestions

Sugestion, opinions and recommendations expressed by the respondents are listed below.

- It is suggested that the library should be introduced the open access system for its users population.
- It is also suggested that internet and automated library services may be given to users of the library.

References

Abifarin (Abimbola), Information Seeking Behaviour of Agricultural Students in Selected Nigerian Universities. *Journals of Library of Information Sciences*, Vol. 19, No. 2, December 1994.

Awogbami (PA), Teaching Faculty Members' Perceptions of Librarians : A Survey, *International Library Movement*, 17:1995; 45-51.

Bhattacharya, G., *Information Science : A Unified View at Through a System Approach*, Calcutta, IASLIC, 1987, p. 18.

Buckland, Michael K., Information as Thing, *Journal of the American Society for Information Science*, 42(5), 1991, p. 351.

Cronin (B), Assessing User Needs. *Aslib Proceedings*, 33:1981, pp. 37-47.

Davis, G.B., *Management Information Systems*, New York : McGraw-Hill, 1974, p. 32.

Desh Mukh (GR) Users Survey of Soil Conservation Research Institute Library, *Annals of Library Science and Documents*. 1983, 30(1), pp. 31-34.

Ellis (D) (*et. al.*) "A Comparison of the Information Seeking Patterns of Researchers in the Physical and Social Sciences", *Journal of Documentation*. 49 (4), (1993) 356-69.

Ford, G., *User Studies : An Introductory and Select Bibliography*, Sheffield : for Research on User Studies, 1977.

Ford, G., "Research in User behaviours in University Libraries." *Journal of Documentation*, March 1973, 29(1) : 85-106.

Garg, Kailash (Chandra) and Ashok Kumar, *Information Gathering Habits of R & D Scientist : A Survey Annals of Library Science Documentation*. Vol. 31, Numbers 1-2, March-June, pp. 63-73.

Geetha (Balasubramaniyan) and Biswas (SC), *Readers and their Reading Trends in the British Council Library*, Delhi Annals of Library Science and Documentation, 1980, 27 (1-4), 66-77.

Herner (S), The Information-Gathering Habits of American Medical Scientists. *In Proceedings of the International Conference of Scientific Information*. National Academy of Science. The Academy, Washington DC, Vols. 16-230.

Jasmer Single and Hari Single, Needs and Expectations of Users from a University Library, *Indian Journal of Information, Library and Society,* 6 : 1993; 219-30.

Kawatra (PS), Attitudes of Research Scholars Towards the Resources and Services of three University Libraries in Rajasthan (India). *A Study Annals of Library Science and Documentation.* 35 : 1988 : 171-77.

Kent, A.K., Information as Power, *ASLIB Proceedings,* 31(1), 1979, p. 16.

Koblitz, J., Librarianship and Documentation Information : Distinctive Features and Common Aspects. In : *On Theoretical Problems Information,* Moscow : All-Union Institute for Scientific and Technological Information, 1969, pp. 120-42.

Krishan Kumar, "Users' Survey Concerning Teachers and Research Scholars in the Department of Chemistry, University of Delhi", *Annals of Library Science,* December, 1968, 15(4) : 175-207.

Line, M.B., Draft definitions : Information and Library Needs Wants, Demands and User. *ASLIB Proceedings,* 26, 1974; p. 87.

Line, M.B. *The entry for the word NEED in Encyclopedia of psychology,* edited by H.J. Eysenck, W. Arnold, R. Maili, London : Search Press, 1972.

Mallaiah (TY) and Badami (KK), Library and Information Services Facilities in Mangalore University Library from the research Scholar's View : A Survey. *Annals of Library Science and Documentation,* 40; 1993; 155-165.

Menzel, H., *Review of Studies in the Flow of Information among Scientists,* 2 Vols. New York : Columbia University, Bureau of Applied Social Research, 1960.

———, *Information needs and users in Science and Technology.* ARIST. 1; 1966; 41 - 69.

Panwar (BS) and Vyas (SD) user Survey of the Women College Library Library Herald of Library Science, Vol. 15, NI, January 1979, 3-34.

Paisley, W.J., The Flow of (Behavioural) *Science Information—A Review of the Research Literature,* Palo Alto Cal : Standard University, 1965.

Prasad (HN) and Tripathi (Manorama), Information Seeking Behaviours of Physical Sciences and Social Scientists : A report. *Annals of Library Science and Documentation,*Vol. 45, No. 2, June 1998; 41-48.

Rolinso (H) : Information Use Pattern of Scientists; *Annals of Library Science and Documents.* 38(2) (1995), 32-40.

Sathyanarayana (M), Information Needs Planning on Effective Library, Indian Journals of Information and Library, *Journal of Information and Library Science,* Vol. 10, Nos. 1-2, January-June, 1997.

Sasikala (C), Information Seeking Behaviour of Managers in Industry, *IASLIC Bulletin*, 39 : 1994 : 27-31.

Sethi (AR), *Information Seeking Behaviour of Social Scientists; An Indian Perspective*, 1990. Hindustan Publication Company, Delhi.

Sudharani (DV) and Veeranjaneyulu (K), Information Use : A Survey of the Faculty Members of Sri Padmavathi Mahila Viswavidyalayam (SPMVU), Tirupathi (AP). *Indian Journal of Information and Science*. Vol. 12, 3-4, July-December 1999. 219-25.

Vital Rao (D), *Information Seeking Behaviour of Users—A Case Study of the Scientific at National Institute of Nutrition*, Hyderabad. Lucknow Librarian 10.

Wysoki, A., *A Study of Users Information Needs : Subject and methods in International Federation fbr Documentation on Theoretical Problems of Informatics*. Moscow, All. Union Institute for Scientific and Technical Information, 1989.

Royal Society Scientific Information Conference, London, 1946. *Report and Papers submitted*, London; Royal Society, 1978.

The Oxford English Dictionary, Oxford : The Clarendon Press, 1989, Vol. 7, p. 944.

2

Information Seeking Behaviour

INTRODUCTION

It is not surprising to realize that has always been interested in information in the production, consumption and dissemination. Information has been described as the fifth need of man ranking after air, water, food and shelter. In one form or the other, it has consistently been a significant element in the development of human society and it has shaped over a long period of time into the way in which we think and act. It is likely, of course, to continue to do so with even greater intensity. Information in particular becomes more meaningful when it is transferred and communicated. In other words, information is activated by communication.

The purpose of transfer and communication of informations of 'use' without the intention on the part of the ultimate receiver of beneficiary of information to use it. The whole exercise of transfer and communication become futile and information transferred becomes redundant. On the other hand, seeking and communicating information are two sides of the same coin from the view point of individuals concerned.

Both have the same purpose and use. Information, which has no use, is not information. Thus the central thread of the communication is 'use'. Hence the emphasis is on use and user orientation to communication and information whether from a formally designed and operated information system or from an informal source. A wide range of research works have centered around use and user of information called use and studies have cropped up in the last four decades.

The user is the key person seeks information of any library. All the luxuries of information, revolution, and problems of information explosion centre around the user and his convenience. Understanding the user is half the battle in providing information services. The success of any library depends considerably on how best the system design is based on a close and accurate understanding of the users. The user is not only the most important aspect, but is also, paradoxically, a dynamic component of the library. As such, understanding the user is an important and a continuous activity, know the customer is a cardinal rule of lay business enterprise.

Accordingly, extensive market research, customer behaviour studies and demand forecasting are carried out in business. A formal information center or library is yet to pick up these activates in the sample spirit. Hence it is necessary to know the information needs, the movies and purpose of seeking information, ways and means of gathering information and the entire user-attitudes and practices in relation to information.

More research into behaviour and information gathering patterns of the user groups, will assist the library more effectively in developing programmes and using the resource and limited funds to achieve desired goals. Accurate and up-to-date knowledge about users and their information behaviour is one of the essential ingredients for any library system design.

The effectiveness of library and information system depends on the extent to which the system's characteristics correspond with the user and on how much potential the user is willing and able to make use of it. Hence the design of any library system is to be based on a proper understanding of the user. In this way, only a librarian can improve upon his role as an information transfer agent. He has to intimately and individually understand the requirements of his users and continuously update his knowledge about users through systematic studies and observations.

Information seeking behaviour studies is one of the important areas information users studies. The motives and purpose of uses give rise to information needs and requirements. To satisfy such needs and requirements, users adopt many ways and means of accessing and searching sources of information.

Then they try to acquire necessary information both regularly and other way as necessary from these sources of predetermined. Thus leading to satisfaction or dissatisfaction information relation to purpose and needs.

User Study

User study means the systematic examination of the characteristics and behaviour of the user of the information systems. It is directly linked with the effectiveness of library and information services as they aim at satisfaction of user needs. The term 'user study' mainly focuses on 'users' to measure their information needs, information seeking behaviour and use pattern.

The term user studies has been defined variously by different information scientists. According to Wysoki, user studies or use studies could be concerned with studying information processing activities of the users. Empirical studies of the use of demand or need for information are usually called user studies 2. The working definition of user study adopted by Centre for Research on user is that be general objectives of research on users is to provide further understanding of the processes of information transfer.

The research may be expected to lead to the improvement of information transfer system of all types and to have implications for the organization of communication, the distribution of researcher and the relationships between systems. Information in the light of the above definition a study which is focussed on users to understand directly or indirectly their information needs, use behaviours and use pattern is usually called user study.

User studies are being conducted on the behaviour of the user information seeking information instead of the needs of the user. These studies are more useful to study the user, his psychology, the working conditions, the impact of his position information the society, etc. With this, the user group is studied information a better way to modify the services and tools of the information system.

According to Wysoki, user studies or use studies, could be concerned with studying information processing activities of the users.

Information Seeking Behaviour

The users may seek information in a number of ways such as reading books, browsing periodicals, consulting abstracts and indexing periodicals, contacting colleagues and friends, seeking information from library and information centers and attending seminars, conference, etc.

The studies to find out how a user seeks his information may help the library authorities to organize their acquisition programmes effectively and to introduce appropriate service.

Information seeking is a behaviour of human activity such as writing, a men driving a car or talking on the phone. Since certain items from sources common to all behaviour, psychologist to determine why people do what they do.

Information seeking behaviour is an area of active interest among librarians and information scientists. It results from the circumstances and from a variety of sources. Recognition of some need perceived by user who, as a consequence makes demand upon formal system such as librarians, information centre's on-line services or some other person information order to satisfy the perceived need.

Information seeking behaviour can be defined as a process of constructions in which a user processes from uncertainty (or confusion) to understanding (or clarity). It is an experience with thoughts, actions, and feelings interwoven into a complete mosaic rather in a separate distinct entity.

Information seeking behaviour includes actions or strategies undertaken to locate information. It is the recognition of some need perceived by the user who as a result make demand upon a library and information system or some other individual in order to meet his information requirement.

The field is composed of studies that are concerned with who needs what kind of information and for what reasons and how their need can be identified and satisfied. The information seeking behaviour is thus concerned with establishing relationship with people, information and system of an order so as to obtain the best results.

Definition

According to Kritelas, information seeking behaviour refers to "any activity of an individual that is undertaken to identify a message that satisfies a perceived need".

King defined the information seeking behaviour as "a manner information which a user conducts himself in relation to a given information environment". It is therefore, regarded as essentially, a process of interaction between the use and the rest of the information system.

Girja Kumar has emphasized that the information seeking behaviour is mainly concerned with need, what kind of information and for what reason; how information is found, evaluated and used, and how the needs can be identified and satisfied. According to him, the following processes take place in the information seeking behaviour.

- Identifying the objective
- Defining the need
- Accessing information system
- Establishing sources of information
- Information acquisition
- Use of information
- Satisfaction/dissatisfaction

Types of Information Seeking Behaviour

Information seeking behaviour falls into two types, namely :

1. Compulsory Information Seeking, and
2. Discretionary Information Seeking.

1. Compulsory Information Seeking

Compelling statutes persuade one to seek information necessarily. In many cases a person risks a penalty for not finding information that is known to be in a source. For example a lawyer has to obtain legal information regarding his case and in this case information seeking becomes a compulsory activity. In any case a lawyer cannot afford to miss or fail to locate the required information.

2. Discretionary Information Seeking

This type is different from compulsory information seeking. It entails searching for information that may not be essential and/or whose source is not know with certainly. Not locating the information may lead to serious consequences. In such cases a user can do away with the seeking of such information. Whatever be the type of information seeking, the environmental factors play a vital role information motivating a user either to seek or not to seek information uninfluenced by the creators of the information.

According to Stephen E. Wilberly and report Allen Daugherty "Numerous factors impinge on the persistence of users. Most of these factors are beyond the influence of these who create information sources.

This is one side of the information seeking behaviour. The other side of the coin is the psychology of users as influenced by the external environment to the library. A motivated person goes to seek his information from various sources including those in a library.

Elements of Information Seeking Behaviour

Information seeking is a matter or less related to the sense making information which the individual chases an in-depth one item of information that best fits to his needs and purpose.

Making an in-depth study on "Information needs", Derivn Nilan have proposed a paradigm shift for information seeking behaviour. They have identified an automotive set of premises and assumptions the essence of alternative paradigm information a set of six elements. They are:

1. The conception of information as objectives *versus* subjective.
2. Information users as passive recipient or objective information *versus* purposive self-controlling and centre making beings.
3. User of information behaviour applied cross situations *versus* behaviour understood as the result of dialogue between system and user in which need articulation goes through situation and bound interactions.
4. The study of user behaviour primarily information the context of user interaction with the system *versus* holistic approaches that focus on the whole social interaction.

5. Focus on external behaviour *versus* internal congestion.
6. Concerns that a focus on individual behaviour yields too much variation for system to integrate versus the need, with individually information user behaviour. They however, conclude that traditional approaches have aspired to sophisticated quantitative techniques, yet information the context of the impetus of the paradigm shifts, scholars are now calling for supplementing quantitative approaches with indicatives and qualitative approaches.

REVIEW OF LITERATURE

A study has been made by Herner on 450 medical scientists on the use of formal and informal channels of communication results show that the majority medical scientists got the idea of new project through personal contacts discussions with their colleagues and the remaining got from their own personal work.

Chris Mulder the librarians of two Western Australian colleges of advanced education have combined to carry out surveys of students' attitudes to their respective college libraries. Both colleges have substantial teacher education programmes, have similar enrolments and library holdings, yet library use patterns differ significantly between them.

Garg and Ashok Kumar carried out study on information gathering habits of R & D scientists, viz., physicists, chemists and mathematicians using a questionnaire.

A study was conducted by Barua and Tripatti on the research scholars of Burdwan University to know their information needs, information source used by them, various approaches of information, problems of access to information and various services provided by the university library.

Sethi has made a study on information seeking behaviour of social scientists. Result indicated that they did not differ in respect to how they seek their information in their choice of channels and sources of information. The information seeking behaviour of social scientists, information developing and developed countries tend to be different on account of differences of information the social systems. Infrastructure for collection is the storage utilization of information.

Premsmit investigated the information needs of academic medical scientists of Chulalong Koran University information, Bangkok, Thailand. Results indicated that the scientists need up-to-date information relating to their interest and information on new research findings.

Malhotra carried out a study on the postgraduate students of Haryana Agricultural University and Punjab Agricultural University to know the use of the library and adequacy of library collection in meeting their information requirements.

A study was conducted by Acamma on the scientists of Rubber Research Institute to know their information need and use pattern of information sources.

A study was conducted by Ahanenc to examine the use of libraries and information centers by the administrative and decision-makers of the lmo state, Nigeria.

A study was undertaken by Allen to determine the patterns of library use of the international student's population.

A study conducted by Curtis and Hurd on information seeking behaviour including use of major bibliographic tools by faculty members at the Illinois University at Chicago revealed that over 70% of the faculty used index medicus of MEDLINE. It was also found that there was a wide variation of information the number and format of secondary services used by faculty. The study recommended that training sessions are to be conducted for the users on how to use formats of bibliographic tools.

A study was conducted by Reddy and others to assess the faculty satisfaction with the periodical collection of the library of University of Hyderabad. The results of the study revealed that a majority of faculty were not satisfied with the periodicals collection.

Sasikala conducted a study to know the information seeking behaviour of managers working information 20 industrial organizations of Andhra Pradesh using a questionnaire. Some differences are found in their information seeking behaviour among the senior, middle and junior managers.

Abifarian says that the most of the students do not know how to use the library catalogue, which is the key to holding of each library. Their reason for this is, that it is time consuming and information the end not useful. They used to organize in-service training for library assistant to equip than with the challenges associated with their duties in order to be more useful to students.

Lzah studied on information needs and seeking behaviour on extension specialists and technical officers of National Agricultural Extention and Research Liasion on services at Ahmadu Bello University using the questionnaire method. The study revealed the various ways information which the information was sought.

Lalitha conducted a study on information seeking behaviour or medical and engineering personnel. The information in any field is required to update the knowledge of seeks. The study is especially in case practitioners of applied sciences and technologies.

The present survey for the information seeking habits of medical and engineering personal at different level students, teachers practitioners and research workers are studied. Both the formal and informal approaches to collect information, as practiced by the two communities of students.

Ellis analysed the information seeking behaviour among social scientists, then discussed the use of electronic communication through electronic database and computer-based information online search.

Adedibu and Adio studied on the information needs and information seeking patterns of medical students at Latch,

Ogbomoso using a questionnaire method. The survey revealed that 70 percent of respondents spent 3.8 hours per week in the library consulting books relevant to their areas of specialization, and 68 percent of this category approached the library staff for assistance information searching the books of their choice. All of the sample agreed that the library staff are always willing to assist. Various suggestions were made by the respondents for the improvement of the library.

Alkinson and Figueroa investigated the library use and research behaviour of business students at California State University at San Macros by selecting a sample of 159 students.

Bawden and Robinson conducted a study on the information need and information seeking behaviour of nurses. The study mainly conducted by semi structured interviews with them shows midwifery industry to be particularly information conscious, needing a wide variety of information and psychiatric nurses appear to be much less information conscious.

Curtis and others studied on the information seeking behaviour of health sciences faculty at the Illinois University at Chicago using a questionnaire the study found that the use of the print Index Medicus among faculty was information transition, while 30.5 percent continued to use the print resources, 68.0% of the faculty accessed MEDLINE through electronic means.

Faculty preferred accessing electronic databases from their offices to doing so from the library. Health sciences faculty used a variety of databases, in addition to MEDLINE, to fill their information needs. Most faculties did not take advantages of either houses of electronic training sessions offered by the librarians.

Harikrishna Reddy and Karisidappa's study on information seeking behaviour of 160 professionals in the field of disabilities in India, through a questionnaire method, revealed that informal channels were mostly used for information gathering. Journals were preferred for formal source of information for preparing course/teaching materials. Books were used for providing consultation and offering therapeutic diagnostic services. The time spent in borrowing/ reading literature for various purposes has also been studied.

It is identified that authors like Wilson and streatified (1997) have analysed the information seeking behaviour by taking into account all indicators discussed above viz. use and value of information sources, pattern of library use, information need and use of electronic communication.

Pelzer and others made a study on the library use and information seeking behaviour of veterinary medical students at Iwa State University using a questionnaire method. Results showed that the 1997 students used the library most frequently for photocopying, and studying course work and they preferred text books and hand outs for current information.

However, a majority shift was seen from the use of print indexes and abstract information, 1987 towards the use of computerized indexes and other electronic resources information in 1997. Sixty percent of the students reported that they use the internet for current information.

Overall use of electronic materials was highest among students receiving the problem based learning method of instruction. Most of the 1997 students indicated that the electronic resources would be important for future education needs, particularly the health information and series available of the internet and World Wide Web.

Ziji and Gericke made a study on information seeking patterns of artists and art scholars at the Royal Triangle Technikon, South Africa. The preferred information sources were found to be (in order of preference) periodical articles, library books in private collections, visits to art galleries and the internet. The preferred methods of information seeking were conducting own searches information catalogues or OPACS, asking a librarian and searching for the information seeking references of artists and an increasing interest in electronic media as serious implications for information provides of the future.

Prasad and Tripathi carried out a study based on a sample of 26 physical and social scientists. So the findings can be generalized although the findings provide significant insight into the similarly and differences information the information seeking behaviour of physical and social scientists in India.

Mahaswarappa and Haranur studied the relative importance of information sources among a biological scientists and on the basis of statistical test concludes that the personal attributes of biological scientists such as designation, experience and nature of researching in a university environment have been on the use of information sources.

A survey made by Sudharani and Veeranjaneyulu to know the opinion of most of the faculty members stated that they are satisfied with the services and information for human development of Sri Padmavathi Mahila Viswavidyalayam, Tirupathi.

Biradar and Sampath Kumar in their study attempt to evaluate the service and facilities offered by DVS polytechnics college library, Shimoga. The study shows that 37.5% students and 46.88% teachers are satisfied with lending service and 48.75% students and 46.88% teachers are satisfied with lending service and 48.75% students and 46.88% teachers are satisfied with lending service and 48.75% students and 50% of teachers respectively have a good opinion about the book ban facility of the college library.

Mahapatra and Randa explain theory of ISB at length provides an insight into myriad mines of information seeking behaviour such as its concept associated with psychological attributes, behaviour options and ecological influence, impact of dissonance theory, different methods and categories of information seeking also reflects different models of ISB and their implications along with the findings of some of the useful research carried out by ISB.

A study was carried out by S. Mohamed Esmail and Uma use pattern of information sources by under-graduate students of Engineering Faculty information, Annamalai University. It is observed from the study that under-graduate students heavily depend on books, class notes, popular magazines, newspapers notes of senior students. The other sources are least used by under-graduate students viz., microforms, biographical sources, almanacs, memoranda diaries and letters.

Esmail and others conducted a study on information access pattern of teaching staff and research scholars of Natural Science in Annamalai University. The main aim of the study is to measure the success or failure of the working system of university library and reading habits and variety of interest of the teaching staff and research scholars information in their filed and also it will be a guidance to the librarian to procure the required documents according to the need and interest of the users. The study also determines the national scientists and their level of information sources utilization and level of information services satisfaction by using ranking method of analysis.

RESEARCH DESIGN

For the successful conduct of any research study and meaningful inference, an appropriate methodology is indispensable. The main-focus of this study is to analyse the utilization of college library by the faculties.

Need for the Study

A review of literature reveals that there is no single study have been carried out on information seeking behaviour of faculties.

Hence the main aim of the study is to assess the need and satisfaction of the users of Engineering College library information the view of library resources and services.

Objectives

The following are the major objectives of the present study.

1. To assess the use of information channels.
2. To identify the frequency of visit to library by the faculties of the Engineering college.
3. To identify the purpose for which the faculty visit the library
4. To know the user's satisfaction of library services.
5. To know the user satisfaction regarding library infrastructure facilities.
6. To know the database which are used by faculties in their respective discipline?

Hypothesis

Based on the above mentioned objectives the following hypothesis have been formulated and tested.

There would be significant variation among Professor, Asst. Professors, Senior Lecturer and Lecturer in the following:

1. Formal Communication of Respondents
2. Informal Communication of Respondents
3. Frequency of Visit to Library
4. Purpose of the Visit to the Library
5. Use of Electronic Database and Electronic Journals

Methodology

A study is mainly based on the primary data collected from the faculties through a well designed questionnaire. Besides, the secondary data have been collected from sources like textbooks, medical college prospectus, official guides, reference books, national and international journals and magazines.

Data Collection

The primary data has been collected by using empirical

methods of questionnaire. At first, a pilot study was conducted to test the feelings of the respondents in answering the questions. Then the well tested questionnaire was distributed personally to the faculties of Infant Jesus College of Engineering. Sufficient time was given to the respondents for furnishing the information.

At the time of collecting the filled questionnaire each respondent was requested to offer his comments and opinions on various concepts included in it. Suggestions relating to the improvement of library services are also called for.

In order to study the information seeking behaviour of faculties of Infant Jesus College of Engineering have been chosen. All the faculties are included for the present study. About 115 questionnaire distributed to respondents and received back and response rate is 100%. Out of 115 questionnaires received 20 from Professors, 35 from Assistant Professors, 25 from Senior Lecturers and 35 from Lecturers.

Statistical Tools

The data collected through the questionnaire have been analyzed by using averages, simple percentages, two-way analysis of variances (TWO WAY ANOVA).

Chapter Scheme

The study is mainly organized into two parts, namely:

Part I : Theoretical background, and

Part II : Analysis of data.

Part I

It is divided into the following five chapters keeping in view the objectives of the study:

1. First Chapter gives introduction about user studies and information seeking behaviour of users.

2. Second Chapter deals with earlier studies conducted in this filed that is called Review of Related Literature.

3. Third Chapter deals with need for the study, objectives hypothesis and methodology of data collection.

4. Fourth Chapter deals with origin and development of Infant Jesus College of Engineering and its library.

Part II

1. Fifth Chapter deals with the Results and Discussion of the related factors.

2. Sixth Chapter deals with findings and conclusion.

RESULTS AND DISCUSSION

TABLE 1
Cadre-wise Distribution of the Respondents

Sl. No.	*Cadre*	*No. of Respondents*	*% of the respondents*
1.	Professors	20	17.39
2.	Asst. Professors	35	30.43
3.	Senior Professors	25	21.75
4.	Lecturers	35	30.43
	Total	115	100.00

Table 1 indicate the cadre-wise distribution of respondents. Among the 115 respondents, 20 are Professors, 35 are Asst. Professors, 25 are Senior Lecturers and 35 are Lecturers. It shows 17.39%, 30.43%, 21.75% and 30.43% respectively.

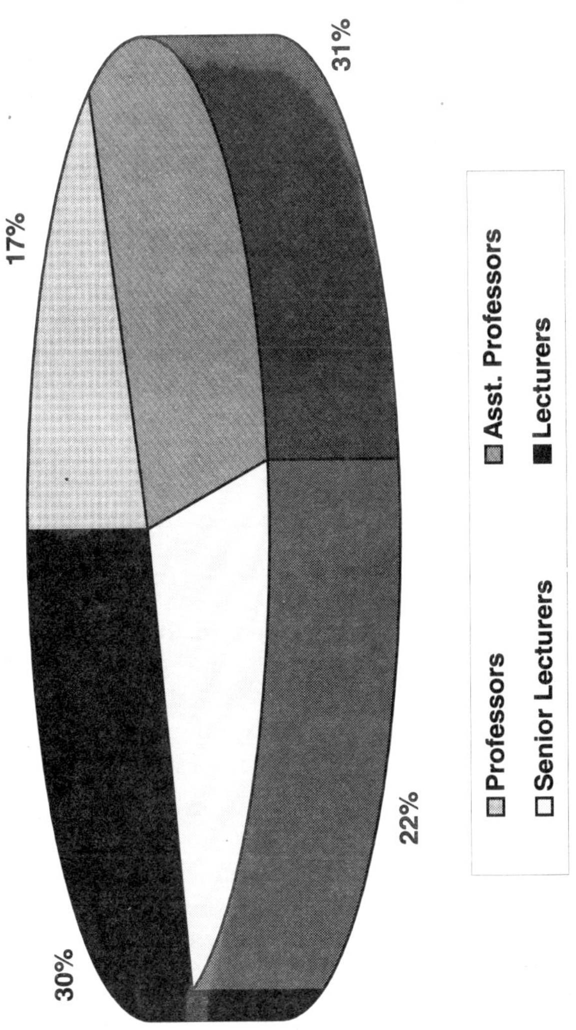
Cadre-wise Distribution of the Respondents
17%
31%
22%
30%
Professors
Asst. Professors
Senior Lecturers
Lecturers

It could be cleared from the above table that Lecturers and Asst. Professors are more compared to other faculties of the college.

TABLE 2
Informal Communication Behaviour of the Respondents

Informal Communication	*Professors*	*Assistant Professors*	*Senior Lecturers*	*Lecturers*	*Total*
No. of national conference symposium/ seminar attended	114	52	38	17	221
No.of international conference symposium/ seminar attended	43	12	10	9	74
No. of times visited foreign countries	28	1	4	1	34
Total	185	72	52	27	329

Informal Communication Behaviour of the Respondents

Table 2 denotes attending national and international conference/symposium/seminars/visiting foreign countries are the major informal communication observed in the present study.

Table 2 indicates 4 types of respondents who have attended number of national conference/symposium/seminar. Out of 221, 114 (51.58%) are by Professors, 52 (23.53%) by Asst. Professors, 38 (17.19%) Senior Lecturers and 17 (7.69%) by Lecturers.

Further it is found that the number of international conference/symposium/seminar attended out of 74, 43 (58.11%) are by Professors, 12 (16.22%) by Asst. Professors, 10 (13.51%) by Senior Lecturers, 9 (12.16%) by Lecturers.

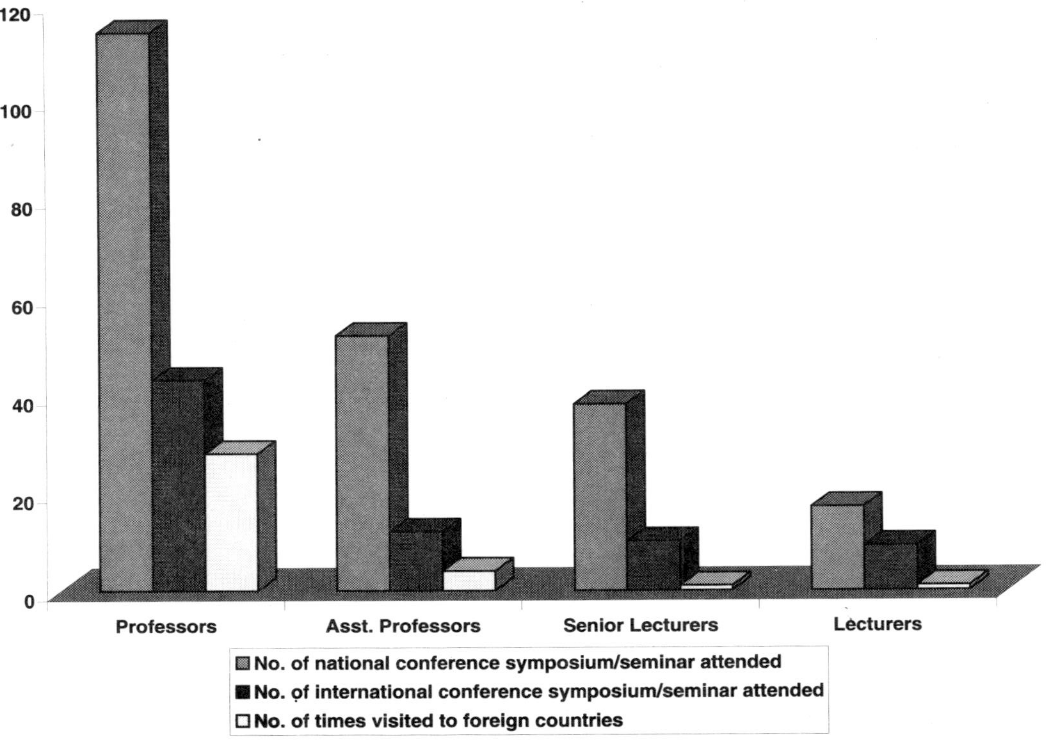
120
100
80
60
40
20
0
Professors
Asst. Professors
Senior Lecturers
Lecturers
No. of national conference symposium/seminar attended
No. of international conference symposium/seminar attended
No. of times visited to foreign countries

As for the number of staff visited to foreign countries, out of 34, 28 (82.53%) by Professors, 4 (11.76%) by Asst. Professors, 1 (2.94%), Senior Lecturer, 1(2.94%) by Lecturers.

In the overall position for informal communication, professor top with 185 (56.23%) followed 68 (20.67%), Asst. Professors, 49(14.89%) by Senior Lecturers and 27 (8.21%) Lecturers.

TABLE 3

Types of Information Needed by the Users

Purpose of	*Professors*	*Assistant Professors*	*Senior Lecturers*	*Lecturers*	*Total*	*Percentage*
Bibliographic Information	18	34	22	32	106	20
Current Information	20	35	24	35	114	22
Retrospective Information	17	32	21	32	102	20
Conceptual Information	16	31	20	29	96	18
Statistical Information	20	35	20	29	104	20
Total	91	167	107	157	522	100

Types of Information Needed by the Users

Table 3 shows that the Information required by the respondents are categorized into five items i.e., bibliographic Information, current Information, retrospective Information, conceptual Information and statistical Information.

Irrespective of the respondents, majority of the respondents (more than 90) required bibliographic conceptual and statistical Information, and below 90% of the respondents required retrospective and conceptual Information.

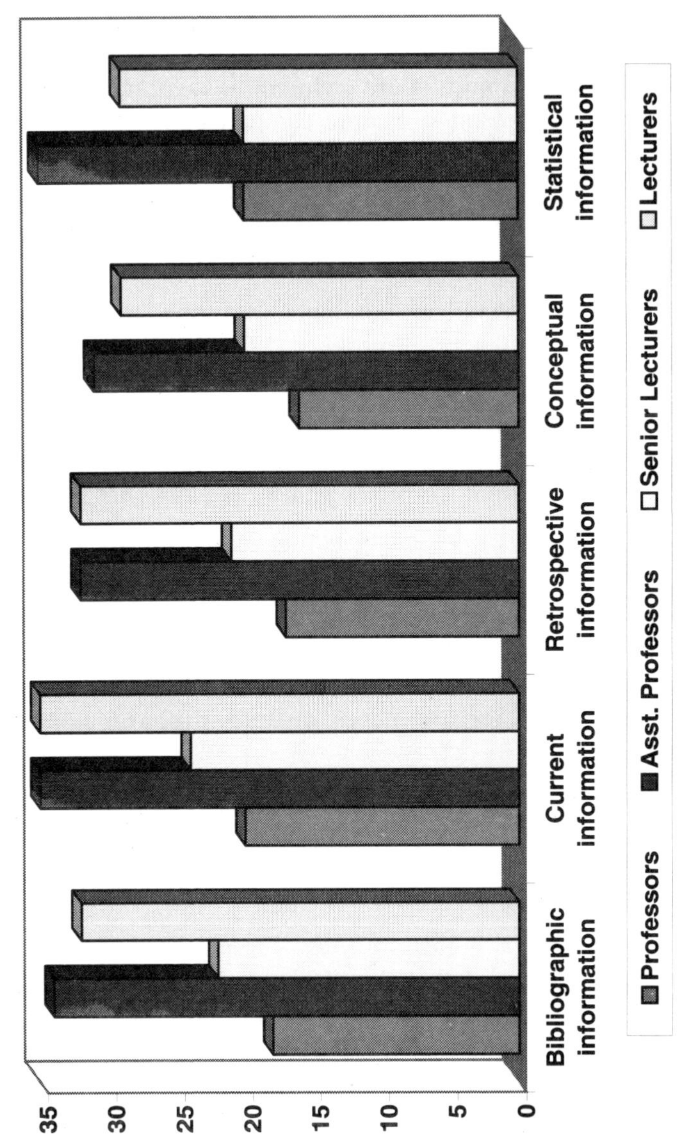
Types of Information Needed by the Users
35
30
25
20
15
10
5
0
Bibliographic information
Current information
Retrospective information
Conceptual information
Statistical information
Professors
Asst. Professors
Senior Lecturers
Lecturers

FINDINGS AND CONCLUSION

The sample population of this study is 115 among them 20 respondents are professors, 35 are Asst. professors, 25 are senior lecturers and 35 are lecturers. It is found that lecturers and asst. professors are more compared to other faculties of the college.

Irrespective of teaching staff majority of the respondents have 6 to 10 years of experience and only 7% of them have above 20 years of experience.

Of the overall respondents in formal communication, professor get first position with 128 (53.33%) followed by 49 (20.42) Asst. Professors, 35 (14.58%) Senior Lecturers and 28 (11.67%) lecturers.

In the overall followed 68 (20.67%) Asst. Professors, 49 (14.89%) by Senior Lecturers and 27 (8.21%) Lecturers.

The majority of the respondents 50 (43.48%) visited the library several times/week, followed 27 (23.48%) once a week, 24 (20.87%) daily 09 (7.93%) once a month and only 5 (4.34%) were visited occasionally.

Majority of respondents visit the library for the purpose of preparing lecture notes and to prepare articles for publication.

All the respondents were satisfied with the services provided by the library except few of them and they did not face any problem while using the library resources to the fullest extent.

Majority of Professors, Asst. Professors, Senior Lecturers and Lecturers said that the library facilities are adequate for preparing lecture notes, setting of assignments, guiding students in regular studies, guiding students for seminar, guiding students for projects and for update professionally.

The adequacy of the reading materials is concerned, Infant Jesus College of Engineering has a good collection. Majority of the respondents from professors, asst. professors, senior lecturers and lecturers they said adequate text book, reference book, books in book bank, periodicals and non-book materials like video cassettes, audio cassettes and CD-ROM is in the library. More than 80% of respondents are satisfied with the collection of resources in the library of Infant Jesus College of Engineering.

Majority of the respondents of Infant Jesus College of Engineering are satisfied by the various library services.

Irrespective of the respondents majority of the respondents (more than 90) required bibliographic conceptual and statistical information and below 90% of the respondents required retrospective and conceptual information.

Most of the respondents said that they are satisfied with the infrastructure, working time and procedures followed by the library.

In lecturer category 42.86% used inspect database, 34.28% used science directs, 22.86% electronic journal. Irrespective of the respondents, more than 48.69% of them used. INSPEC database, 29.57% science directs and 21.74% used electronic journal.

Majority of the respondents satisfied with the CAS service provided in the Infant Jesus College of Engineering library.

Out of the 20 professor, 18 (90%) felt that training is not essential for the use of electronic information followed 29 (82.86%) by Asst. professors, 20 (80%) by Sr. Lecturers and 27 (77.14%) by lecturers. It of reveals that only few of the respondents felt that training is essential for the use of electronic information.

References

Abifarin, Abimbola, 1994. "Information Seeking Behaviour of Agricultural Students in Selected Nigerian Universities". *Journals of Library of Information Sciences*, Vol. 19, No. 2.

Accama, C. *et. al.*, 1991. "Information Needs and use Pattern of Rubber Scientists". *ILA Bulletic*, 36 pp. 89-94.

Adedibu, L.O. and Adioo, G., 1997. "Information needs and Information Seeking Patterns of Medical Students Lnulech Orbomoso". *Aslib Proceedings*, 49 : 238-42.

Ahanene, E.M., 1991. "Use of Library and Information Services in Development Planning Case of Local Government decision maker sin Imo State, Nigeria". *Annals of Library Science and Documentation*, 38 : 74-78.

Allen, M.B., 1993. "Information Students in Academic Libraries : A User Survey", *College and Research Libraries*, 54 : 323-33.

Atkinson, J.D. and Figueroa, M., 1997. "Information Seeking Behaviour in Nursing Specialists : A Case Study of Midwifery". *Journal of Information Science*, 23 : 407-21.

Barua, P. and Tripati, T., 1988. "An Analysis of Information Seeking Behaviour of Research Scholars vis-à-vis Existing Information Sources and Services ofBurdwan University Library : A Case study". *IASLIC Bulletin*, 33 : 93-98.

Biradar, B.S., and B.T. Sampath Kumar, 2000. Evaluation of Information Services and Facilities Offeredby DVS Polytechnic College Library : A Case Study. *Library Heald*, 38 (2) : 112-20.

Bowden, D. and Robinson, K., 1997. Information Behaviour in Nursing Specialities : A Case Study of Midwidery. *Journal of Information Sciences*, 23: 407-21.

Britain, J.M., Information and its users, Bath, Bath University 1970, p. 1.

Chris Mulder, 1981. "Survey of Student Attitudes to Colleges Libraries : Research in Progress is Western Australia". *RUS New*, 10 : 22.

Cronin Blasie, 1981. "Assessing user Needs", *Aslib Proceeding*, 33 (2) : 37-41.

Curtis, K.L. *et. al.*, 1993. Information Seeking Behaviour Survey of Health Science Faculty use of Indexes and Databases". *Bulletin of the Medical Library Association*, 81 : 382-92.

Curtis, K.L. *et. al.*, 1997. Information Seeking Behaviour of Health Sciences Faculty the Impact of New Information Technologies". *Bulletin of the Medical Library Association*, 85 : 402-10.

Ellis, D. *et. al.*, 1996. "A Comparison of the Information Seeking Patterns of Researchers in the Physics and Socio-sciences, *Journal of Documentation*, 49(4), 356-69.

Esmail, Mohamed S., and Uma, V., 2003. Use Pattern of Information Sources by Under-graduate Students of Engineering Faculty in Annamalai University : A Case Study. National Conference on Change Management in Library & Information Science, Organized by Bishop Heber College.

Esmail, Mohamed S., and Uma, V., 2003. Use Pattern of Information Sources by Under-graduate Students of Engineering Faculty in Annamalai University, *Indian Journal of Information Library and Society (IJLIS)*. 17 : 17-26.

Garu, Kailash Chandra and Ashok Kumar, 1984. Information Gathering Habits of R & D Scientists : A Survey", *Annals of Library Science and Documentation*, 31 : 63-73.

Harikrishna Reddy, S., and Karisiddappa, C.R., 1997, "Information Seeking Behaviour : Survey of the Professional in the Field of Disabilities with Special Reference to Mental Handicap in India", *Annals of Library Science and Documentation*, 44 : 64-69.

Hernet, S., The Information Gathering Habits of American Medical Scientists. In Proceeding of the International Conference of Scientific Information. National Academy of Sciences the Academy, Washington, DC. 1959, 16-21.

Izah, Zariam, 1995. "Information Needs and Seeking Behaviour of Extension Specialists and TechnicalOfficers of National Agricultural Extension and Research Liaison Services". *Library Focus*, 13 and 14:50-66.

Lalitha, M. 1995. Information Seeking Behaviour of Medical and Engineering Personnel : A Comparative Study with Reference to their Library use Library Science with Slant to Documentation and Information Studies, 32 (2) : 65-74.

Mahapatra, R.K., and K.C. Randa, 2001. Information Seeking Behaviour : A Conjectural Approach, *SRELS Journal of Information Management*, 38 (2).

Mahapatra, R.K., and K.C. Randa 2001. Information Seeking Behaviour : A Conjectural Approach. *SRELS Journal of Information Management*, 38 (2) : 121-38.

Maheswarappa, B.S. and Havanur, Bagyashree, K. 1998. "Use of Information Sources versus the Personal Attributes of Biological Scientists in a University Environment in India". *Library Science with a Slant Documentation and Information Studies*, 45 : 85-100.

Malhotra, H.P. 1990. "User Studies in Libraries of Agricultural University Meeting the Information Requirements of Post-graduate Students". *Annals of Library Science and Documentation*, 37 : 59-62.

Peizer, N.L. *et. al.* ,1998. "Library use and Information Seeking Behaviour of Veterinary Students Revisited in the Electronic Environment". *Bulletin of the Medical Library Association*, 86 : 346-55.

Prasad, H.N. 1992, Information Need and User, Varanasi. *Indian Bibliographic Centre*, 88-92.

Prasad, H.N., 1992. Information Need and Users, 1992. Indian Bibliographic Centre, Varanasi. p. 76.

Prasad, H.N. and Tripathi, Manorama, 1998. "Information Seeking Behaviour of Physical Scientists and Social Scientists : A Report". *Annals of Library Science and Documentation*, 45 (2) : 41-48.

Premsmit, P., 199C. "Information Needs of Academic Medical Scientists at Chulalongkon University". *Bulletin of the Medicinal Library*, 78 : 383-87.

Reddy, Y.N. *et. al.*, 1993. "Assessment of Faculty Satisfaction with Periodical Collection a Case Study". *Lucknow Librarian*, 25 : 25-31.

Sasikal, C., 1994. "Information Seeking Behaviour of Managers in Industry". *IASLIC Bulletin*, 39 : 27-31.

Sethi, A.R., Information Seeking Behaviour of Social Scientists; An Indian Perspective, 1990. *Hindustan Publication Company*, Delhi.

Sudharani, D.V. and Veeranjaneyulu, K., 1999. Information Use : A Survey of the Faculty Members of Sri Padmavathi Mahila Viswavidyalayam (SPMVU), Tirupathi (AP). *Indian Journal of Information and Science*. 12 (3-4) : 219-25.

Wiberby, Stephen, *et. al.*, 1998. "User Persistence in Scanning Lists of References", *College and Research Libraries*, 15 : 149-51.

Wilson, I.O. and Streatfield, D.R., 1997. "Information need in Local Authority Social Sciences Departments : A Report". *Journal of Documentation*, 334 : 277-93.

Wysoki, A., Study of Users Information Needs, Subject and Methods in International Federation for Documentation on Theoretical Problems of Informatics, Moscow, All. *Union Institute for Scientific and Technical Information*.

Wysoki, A., Study of Users Information Needs, Subject and Methods in FID on Theoretical Problems of Information, Moscow, *All Union Institute for Scientific and Technical Information*.

Zijl, Vanc, and Gericke, E.M., 1998. "Information Seeking Pattern of Artists and Art Scholars at the Vall Triangle Technikon". *South African Journal of Library and Information Science*, 16 : 23-33.

3

Library Utilization

INTRODUCTION

Library as we all know, is a collection of written, printed or other graphical materials organized for use. Library as such is a treasure house preserving the master spirit of great writers embalmed for the posterity. The need for libraries as the central part of educational institution has been recognized since ancient times. In the 20th Century, the college libraries developed rapidly as instruments of teaching, as emphasis in instruction swing from text books through assigned sections of several books to free research in the available literature.

Specialization in all fields necessarily has its counterpart in library service and which public libraries have built up many special collections. There is an insistent demand for the library devoted to a specific subject, even in the expansion of research activity, particularly in science and technology. This has led to phenomenal increase in scientific literature.

The extension of library service into securing the flow of information to the right people has led to parallel development of techniques. Library is now concerned with information, in whatever form Library books, phamphlets, reports and the publications of societies. The electronic component of information technology has paved way for e-library, which has a tremendous online resources flowing into the library with the latest information that is happening around the world.

Thus the modern library is an interactive classroom, computer aided teaching package which is most commonly known as computer based teaching (CBT), is different from the traditional way of classroom teaching or rather its complement the traditional teaching methods with such a greater impact.

In the field of higher education and research, the primary function of a research institute library is to make available important information materials necessary to pursue research and development activities.

In the professional line, library is a vital lifeline for a professional student to cope up with the day-to-day advancement in science and technology. Classroom teaching alone cannot fulfil the requirements that professional student need to achieve in building his knowledge in his area of specialization. It is only the hybrid library that comes to fulfil his requirements.

Competence in the use of library is a combination of attitudes, knowledge and skills. It depends on the awareness of important scientific and technical literature and a desire to use them. Knowledge of the kinds of materials, which the library holds, and the development of skills in locating, selecting, using, describing and evaluating those materials is required.

The use of library especially for professional students, the advent of new storage media, electronic networking of systems, sophistication of programming techniques has contributed to the growing awareness and use of databases in the field of professional subjects.

Since hybrid library has paved the way for interaction, it is more informative and interactive than a classroom. A study on the user behaviour of the hybrid library with respect to time utilization and usage of different components of the hybrid library is the need of the day.

Proper utilization of the available resource is required for the students pursuing professional education to get acquainted with the latest developments and findings around the world. Hence, a study on the utilization behaviour of the Undergraduate and Postgraduate students is required to understand their reading habit, their needs and the difficulties, what they face in the process of retrieving materials for their professional career. This would enable the author to find out ways and means to facilitate the users for user-friendly environment to tap the library resources.

In this context, it is essential to study the different components of a hybrid library such as textbooks, periodicals, reference books, audio-visual resources, digital resources, on-line resources, email, and reprographic services available in the library.

To be more benetral to the students, it is essential to study not only the different components available in the library but also the utilization behaviour of these components by the students.

Hence, this work makes an attempt to investigate the method of library utilization behaviour of the students with the following specific objectives:

1. to assess the time utilization of the students,
2. to study the extent of usage of various components of library,
3. to identify the constraints in the utilization of library by the students, and
4. to make suggestions for effective utilization of the library.

REVIEW OF LITERATURE

Library is a storehouse or rich resource in the form of

books, periodicals, gazetter, yearbook and e-journals including other digital resources. Proper utilization of the available resource is required for the students pursuing professional education to get acquainted with the latest developments and findings around the world. Hence, a study on the utilization behaviour of the Undergraduate and Postgraduate students is required to understand their reading habits, their needs and the difficulties, what they face in the process of retrieving materials for their professional career.

1. Importance of Library

Library is a growing organism, says Dr. S.R. Ranganathan, the father of Library Science. Andal (2001) says that one hour or thirty pages reading is a must for a person in a day to update him in the world of science and information technology. Development in any sphere of life and, more specifically, sustainable development depend primarily on the availability and especially quicker availability of required information says Samyasam (1997).

Any library may not contain all the books published in the world. Resource sharing and co-operation alone could help to overcome this problem says Mc Colvin (1999). Shoaib *et. al.* (1997) point out librarians main role is to act as mediator, liaison in the society by matching the two patterns—the pattern of human thought to the patterns of organization of a library.

Academic libraries support the teaching and research needs of institutions they serve. It is the library's responsibility to ensure that the use of its information sources, resources and services are maximized to benefit its users.

2. Utilization Behaviour of Library Users

Subbiah (1988) spells that the information needs of agricultural students by and large relevant to Indian conditions, which may be of some help in planning the library and information services in agricultural libraries in India.

Agricultural library operations and functions require standardization to provide an effective library and information service says Subbiah (1988).

The role of the academic library has now expanded to encompass multimedia resources and increasingly, full-text digital libraries. As for as the application of information technology in modern academic libraries, computer application for information storage and retrieval provide accuracy and brings an increased ability for information dissemination efficiently from the enormous collection of documents.

3. Hybrid Library

The combination of traditional physical resources and digital material constitute what may be called a Hybrid Library, says Hey (2002). Hey visualizes and examines new problems that arise for information retrieval in current and future academic environments.

Using the Internet in academic services helps the students to download web-based literature. The accessibility in terms of the quality academic services could be achieved by creating web directory in the specific area of study in the library to facilitate the users. Alzamil (2002) highlights the need for the Internet's effect as a delivery tool for academic services. He further spells out that the quality of academic library services. Internet-based academic library services have a significant impact on the educational performance of students taking professional courses. A majority of the professional faculty gave assignments to their students that required the use of library services via., the Internet.

We are now in information age and information society. The foremost characteristic of this era and society is the dependence on and attaching, immense value to information, possibly most important of resources, says Samyasam (1997). Development and more specifically, sustainable development depend primarily on the availability, and especially, quicker availability of required information.

Kaliammal (1999) is of the opinion that we are heading towards an era of paperless library. Web libraries by individuals are freely available through Internet services. The Guttenberg and Oxford Text Archives are pioneers in this project.

Rajalakshmi *et. al.* (1997) highlights the advent of new storage media, electronic networking of systems, sophistication of programming techniques have all contributed to the growing awareness and use of databases in biology and biotechnology.

Donna (2002) in her findings says that managerial support was found to be an instrumental towards the utilization of library in an effective manner. Motivation was an important factor in the library utilization behaviour of the readers.

Clabo's (2002) studies revealed that the utilization behaviour would help to identify materials for purchasing areas in which students need assistance in completing projects or the material what the uses intends to read.

Clabo (2002) finds parents and English teachers were the most influential in encouraging library use, although teachers had more influence on female students than male students. Female students also visited the library on a more frequent basis. The users profile would help the librarian in making long-range plans for their libraries. This research would help to formulate broad based policy making process with more experienced personnel, to make the library user friendly and compatible for the users.

4. Importance of Modern Library

Modern Library is an interactive classroom. Computer Aided teaching package, which most commonly known as Computer Based Teaching (CBT), is different from the traditional way of classroom teaching or rather it complement the traditional teaching methods with a such greater impact. A Computer Assisted Instruction (CAI) tutorial is achieved between computer programme and student, when the responses derived from the programme highly responsive to the question, answers and directives given by the student, while at the same time the dialogue advances the goals and means established by the author of the curriculum materials (Zinn, 1976).

Computer Aided Teaching can be classified as one of the audio-visual materials in education, metaphorically, they can be called Electronic Books says Akkamahadevi *et. al.* (1997).

5. Utilization Behaviour of Library Users

Academic libraries mostly used for academic work purposes and were least used for entertainment, whereas the Internet was mostly used for communication gratification (Al-Harbi, 2002). In the United States, the survey conducted in the Florida State University revealed that the majority of the students depend on Internet resources that academic libraries (Al-Harbi, 2002).

The study also sought to find out whether libraries were connected to the Internet and if connected, indicate how it is used. Eight libraries responded to questions on the Internet. Five of these libraries are connected to the Internet and three are not connected. In three libraries, users have access to e-mail through the library. In all of the eight libraries which responded to the questions on e-mail and the Internet, only one library carry out user instruction on the use of email facilities and no instruction is carried out on the use of the Internet (Babakisi, 1995).

The Internet poses another challenge to the librarians. It affects their job and working practices. According to Bauwens (1993), knowledge of how to navigate the Internet is now becoming a basic requirement for information professionals. This would enable librarians to carry out instruction on the use of Internet. Users need to be introduced to different on-line catalogues and their search procedures.

Currently none of the libraries examined include instruction on the use of the Internet in their user education programmes. Libraries should not only see themselves as users of Internet, but also as provide them with skills needed for effective exploitation of online resources.

Implementation of information technology require some computer literacy for both users and library staff. Respondents were asked to rate the users exposure and knowledge of computers. Thirty two percent of the libraries rated their users as good, 21 percent of the libraries rated them as fair, 5 percent of the libraries rated them as a combination of very good and good. CD-ROMs enable users, to get current information in their subject areas. Training in CD-ROMs searches will enable users to have access to more information. Identification of information in users research areas available elsewhere, gives users a chance to have access to material through inter-library loans and thus promote resource sharing (Babakisi, 1995).

6. Constraints in using e-library

All users are likely to have some conflict caused by common organizational forces in the library environment. Ally and Arokiasamy (2002) proposed the concept of role as the major means of linking the individual and the organizational levels to study the constraints the readers face in the process of acquiring information from the library.

Ally and Arokiasamy (2002) have found that the female respondents have expressed more constraints than the male respondents.

A study in the Nova South Eastern University on the students success in the world wide web retrieving relevant results with respect to end-user, was lack of computer skills and their inability to construct the search statement in the process of information retrieval (Nowicki, 2002)

Information seeking process demonstrates the dynamic and cyclical nature of the information seeking process (Kim, 2002) in a digital library. The extent of usage of digital library facilities by the students gives the picture, where the students stand to download, what he requires in the world deluged with information. There the end user is important in the diffusion process.

This study will help to assess the extent of the usage and expectation of the users. This study expands our notions about computer and computer literacy to formulate syllabus or orient the students to familiarize towards the effective use of electronic library.

The study of the pattern use of information by students is an important means by which one may understand and identify the information need of Agricultural students says, Subbaiah (1988).

Based on the forgoing review, two dependent variables namely, time utilization behaviour of the students and usage of different components of library were identify for the study purpose. Similarly, appropriate independent variables which may affect the time utilization behaviour of the students as well as the usage of different components of library were also identified. Thus seven independent variables namely, age, educational level, rural/urban background, medium of instruction at school, educational level of parents, annual income of the family and community were selected for the study. The study also aimed that to find out the relationship between the selected independent and dependent variables. Based on the literature available on the constraints in library usage, the study was also aimed that to find out the different problems faced by the students in utilizing the library as well as their suggestions to overcome the problem.

RESEARCH DESIGN

The study entitled, Library Utilization behaviour of the students has the following specific objectives.

Objectives

The specific objectives of the study are as follows:

1. To study the profile of students of College and Research Institute, Killikulam.
2. To assess the time utilization behaviour of students.
3. To study the extent of usage of various components of library.
4. To identify the constraints in the utilization of library by the students.
5. To make suggestion for effective utilization of the library.

Hypothesis

In order to study the above framed objectives, the following hypothesis have been framed and these are tested by applying the appropriate statistical tools.

H1 : There will be significant difference on the characteristics of male and female students.

H2 : There will be difference in the time utilization behaviour of male and female students.

H3 : There will be effective utilization of different components of library.

H4 : There will be relationship between characteristics variables and time utilization behaviour.

H5 : There will be relationship between characteristics variable and usage of different components of library.

This chapter deals with a brief description about the research techniques used in the study under the following sub-heads:

1. Location of the area of the Research
2. Selection of Respondents
3. Selection of variables

4. Collection and Analysis of Data
5. Statistical tools used

1. Location of the area of Research

The study was conducted at Agricultural College and Research Institute, Killikulam in Thoothukudi District of Tamil Nadu. The Agricultural College, Killikulam was established in 1984-85 as the third constituent college of Tamil Nadu Agricultural University, Coimbatore. This Institution was upgraded as Agricultural College and Research Institute in 1989. Since then, it caters to the needs of farming community of Tirunelveli, Tuticorin and Kanyakumari districts. The thrust on research received a further fill up, when the college was elevated as Post-graduate Institution in 1990. In this college B.Sc. (Agri.) a four years Under Graduate progrmme and M.Sc. (Agri), a two years post graduate programme in major disciplines such as Agronomy, Plant Breedings and Genetics, Soil Science and Agricultural Chemistry, Agri. Entomology and Plant Pathology are being offered. The library is provided with 7280 text books in 15 major subjects in Agriculture, 55 periodicals, 5 vernacular journals and 6 leading newspapers. The library is also provided with the needed components of the Hybrid library such as audio-visual resources, digital resources, Internet facility, e-mail facility and reprographic services. An annual budget of approximately Rs. 0.5 lakh is being allotted.

Methodology

2. Selection of Respondents

The students sanctioned strength of B.Sc. (Agri.) programme at Agricultural College and Research Institute, Killikulam is 100 per year. Thus the total strength is 400 for Under Graduate programme. Since it was very difficult to cover the entire population for the study purpose, it was decided to take 25 percent of the population as sample for the study. Thus 100 students studying in the under graduate programme were selected as the respondents. Since the study aimed to compare the gender differences, respondents were selected based on proportionate random sampling method. Regarding M.Sc. (Agri.) degree programme, all the students were selected as respondents for the study. Thus totally 140 students were contacted for the study purpose.

3. Selection of Variables

By perusal of past researches, seven independent variables viz., age, sex, rural/urban background, medium of instruction at school, educational level of parents, annual income of parents, community and two dependent variables viz., time utilization behaviour and usage of different components of library were selected for the study.

4. Collection of Analysis of Data

4.1. Data Collection Tool

The data were collected using a well-structured pre-tested interview schedule. The schedule consisted of five major parts. The part 1 dealt with student's profile. The part 2 dealt with time utilization behaviour of students. The part 3 dealt with usage of various components of library such as textbooks, periodicals, reference books, audio-visual resources, digital resources, e-mail and reprographic service. The part 4 dealt with constraints in the utilization of library and the part 5 dealt with the suggestions for effective utilization of library.

4.2. Period of Data Collection

The data were collected during March and April 2003, by personal interview.

4.3. Analysis of Data

On completion of data collection, the collected data were

coded, processed and tabulated to make the findings meaningful. Then the relevant inferences and conclusions were drawn.

5. Statistical Tools Used

The following statistical tools were used in this study:

a. Percentage analysis
b. Cumulative frequency
c. Correlation coefficient
d. Wilcoxon signed rank test

6. Concept Clarification

1. Library Utilization Behaviour

It is the actual time spent by the students in the library and in this study it is measured in hours, the student respondents spent in a month.

2. Usage of Different Components of Library

It refers to the frequency of usage of different components namely, text books, periodicals, digital resources, on-line resources, audio-visual resources, reference books and reprographic services by the students respondents. In this study it is measured by using a four points continuum ranging from frequently to never.

7. Limitations of Study

The present investigation suffered from the limitations of time and other physical facilities commonly faced by a single researcher. It is a qualitative study based on views expressed by the students for a set pattern of questions. Even though there is a possibility to go in depths in male/female differences and rural/urban differences in library utilization, only a few major areas have been covered on these lines due to time limitation. Inspite of these limitations, every effort was made by the researcher to keep this study as objective as possible by deliberately following all the norms of scientific research.

ANALYSIS

TABLE 1

Overall Usage of Different Components of Library

Sl. No.	*Library Usage*	*Number*	*Percentage*
1.	Low	54	38.57
2.	Medium	67	47.86
3.	High	19	13.57
	Total	140	100

It is evident from Table 1 that the respondents used the various components of library at medium level (47.86%) and 38.57% of respondents who used the library at low level. Only 13.57% of the respondents used the library at high level. It is also evident from the table that a majority of 86.43% of the respondents used the different components of library from low to medium level only.

To study the relationship of characteristic with the usage of different components of library by the respondents, correlation coefficient was worked out and is presented in Table 1.

Table 2 reveals that nearly four fifths of the respondents (78.57%) used the textbooks available in the library at low to medium level only and 21.43% of students used at high level (Figure 2).

The subjectwise extent of usage of textbooks in the library by the students was analyzed and is presented in Table 2.

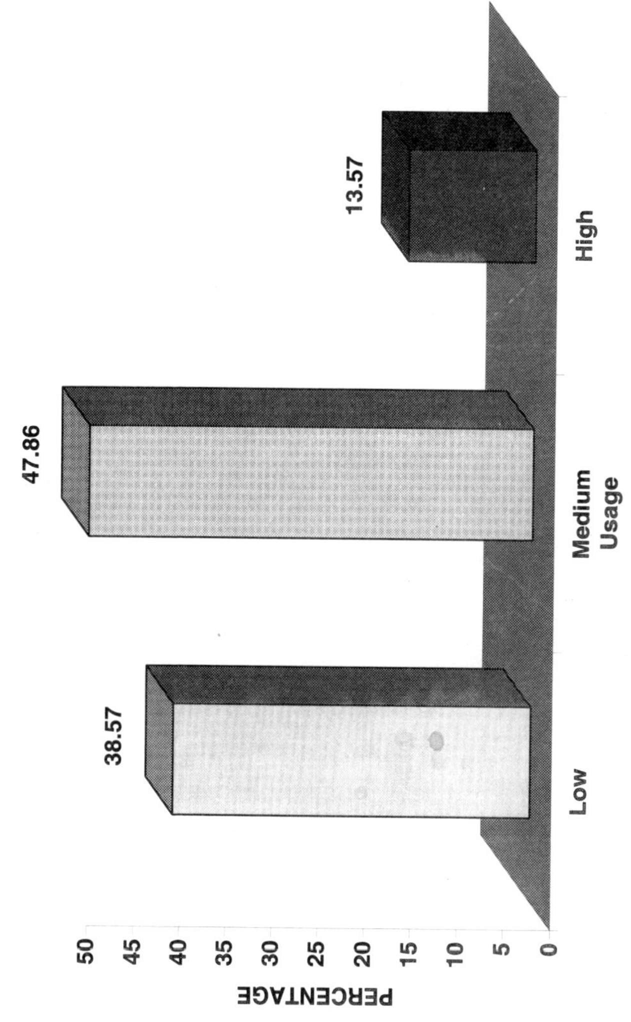

FIG. 1
Overall Usage of Different Components of Library (Percentage)

TABLE 2
Overall Usage of Textbooks in the Library

(n=140)

Sl. No.	*Textbook Usage*	*Number*	*Percentage*
1.	Low	32	22.86
2.	Medium	78	55.71
3.	High	30	21.43
	Total	140	100.00

FIG. 2
Overall Usage of Textbooks in the Library (Percentage)

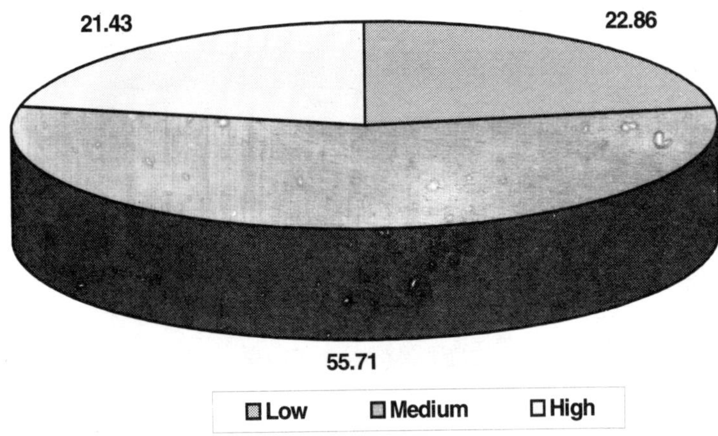

TABLE 3
Overall Usage of Periodicals in the Library

Sl. No.	*Periodical*	*Usage Number*	*Percentage*
1.	Low	59	42.14
2.	Medium	62	44.29
3.	High	19	13.57
	Total	140	100.00

FIG. 3
Overall Usage of Periodicals in the Library (Percentage)

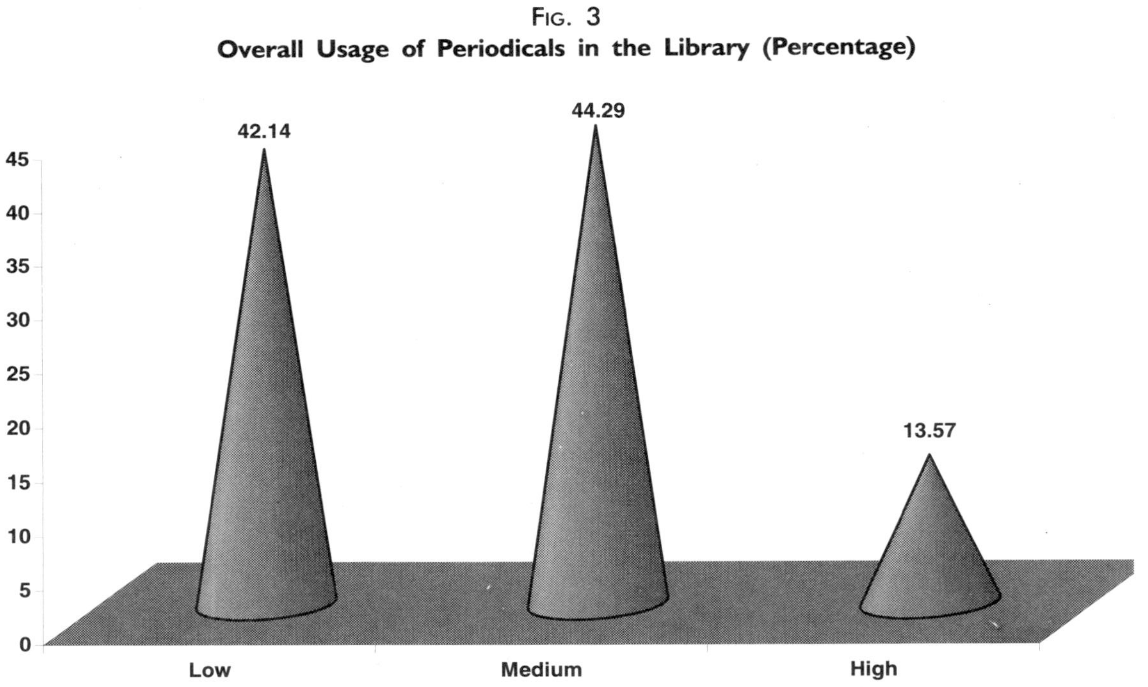

The overall usage of periodicals by the students was analyzed and it is found that most of the students (86.43%) had only low to medium level of usage. Only 13.57% had high level of usage.

To study the relationship of characteristic with the usage of periodicals in the library by the respondents, correlation coefficient was worked out and is presented in Table 3.

FINDINGS AND SUGGESTIONS

The major findings of the study along with the suggestions are presented in this chapter in the following sub-heads.

1. Profile of students
2. Time utilizati0on behaviour of the students
    - 2.1. Frequency of library usage by students
    - 2.2. Time utilization at the library
3. Extent of usage of various components of library
    - 3.1. Overall usage of different components of library
    - 3.2. Usage of textbooks in the library
    - 3.3. Usage of periodicals in the library
        - 3.3.1. Usage of international journals in the library
        - 3.3.2. Usage of national journals in the library
        - 3.3.3. Usage of vernacular journals in the library
        - 3.3.4. Usage of newspapers in the library
    - 3.4. Usage of reference books in the library
    - 3.5. Usage of audio-visual resources in the library
    - 3.6. Usage of digital resources in the library
    - 3.7. Usage of on-line resources in the library
    - 3.8. Usage of reprographic services in the library

4. Constraints in the utilization of library by the students
5. Suggestions for effective utilization of library

I. Profile of Students

The profile of the respondents was analyzed and the major findings are given below:

- All the respondents were young aged.
- About 71.42 percent of the students were studying in B.Sc. (Ag.) and 28.58% were studying M.Sc. (Ag.).
- A majority of 72.14% of students were having rural background and 27.86% were having urban background.
- Among the students hailed from urban area nearly three fourths were females and the remaining one fourth were males.
- Nearly four fifths (79.29%) of the respondents studied in Tamil medium and exactly one fifth (20%) studied in English medium.
- As far as the Tamil Medium is concerned 48.65% of male respondents and 51.35% of female respondents were from tamil medium.
- As for as English medium is concerned more than two thirds (67.86%) of female respondents and less than one-third of male respondents (32.14%) were from English medium.
- About 64.29% of the respondent's parents were educated and 35.71% of the respondents parents were uneducated.
- As regards to male respondents, 54.69% of their parents were educated and 45.31% of the parents were uneducated.
- Whereas in the case of female students 72.37% of

their parents were educated and 27.63% of their parents were uneducated.

- About three fourths (75.01%) of the respondents were having less than Rs. 50,000 as annual income.
- About three fourths (74.29%) of the respondents belonged to either BC or SC/ST.
- Most of the students belonged to Hindu religion.

2. Time Utilization Behaviour of the Students

The time utilization behaviour of the students in the library was analyzed and the major findings narrated below.

2.1. Frequency of Library Usage by Students

- About 55% of the respondents visited the library frequently and 41.42% visited the library occasionally.
- About 53.95% of female students visited the library frequently and 44.74% of the visited library occasionally.
- About 56.25% of male students visited the library frequently and 37.50% of the visited library occasionally.

2.2. Time Utilization at the Library

- More than two thirds of respondents (69.48%) spent 10 to 30 hours per month in the library.
- Regarding female students, exactly half of the respondents spent 20-30 hours in the library per month.
- Regarding male students 71.78% spent 10-30 hours per month in the library.

- ❖ Out of seven characteristics studied, only age and medium of instruction at school were positively and significantly associated with time utilization behaviour.

3. Extent of Usage of Various Components of Library

3.1. Overall Usage of Different Components of Library

A majority of 86.43% of the respondents used the different components of library from low to medium level only.

3.2. Usage of Textbooks in the Library

Nearly four fifths o the respondents (78.77%) used the text books available in the library at low to medium level.

More than fifty percent of the respondents used the text books either frequently or occasionally on the subjects like Agronomy (75%), Plant Pathology (64.29%), Soil Science and Agricultural Chemistry (62.15%), Plant Breeding and Genetics (61.43%), Horticulture (57.85%) and Agricultural Entomology (57.15%).

Textbooks on Agronomy were used more followed by Plant Pathology and Soil Science and Agricultural Chemistry.

The text books on Food Science, Agricultural Statistics and Environmental Sciences were least used by the students.

Only one characteristic viz. age was negatively and significantly related at one percent level of probability with the usage of text books in the library.

3.3. Overall Usage of Periodicals in the Library

The Overall usage of periodicals by the students was analyzed and it is found that most of the students (86.43%) had only low to medium level of usage.

Out of 7 correlation values studied, only one characteristics viz. age was positively and significantly related at one percent level of probability with the usage of periodicals in the library and the variable community was negatively and significantly related at one percent level of probability.

3.3.1. Usage of International Journals in the Library

Most of the respondents (87.88%) had low to medium level of usage regarding International Journals in the library.

Out of 13 International journals available in the library nine journals were used frequently or occasionally by one third of the respondents and the remaining four journals were never used by more than half of the respondents.

The international journals like Rice Abstracts. Plant Breeding Abstracts and Field Crop Abstracts were mostly used by the students and the journals like Agricultural Economics. Seed Abstracts and Seed Science and Technology were least used.

3.3.2. Usage of National Journals in the Library

Majority of the respondents (86.43%) had low to medium level of usage of national journals.

Out of 47 national journals subscribed in the library, 15 journals were used frequently or occasionally by the students, two journals were occasionally or rarely used by more than 60 percent of respondents, 29 journals were never used by more than 40 percent of respondents, and the back volumes of journals were never used by more than half of the respondents.

The above table reveals that the national journals like Kisan World. Indian Journal of Agronomy and Current Science were mostly used by the students and the journals like Review of Devt. And Change. Clay research and journal of Potassium Research were least used.

3.3.3. Usage of Vernacular Journals in the Library

Regarding the usage of vernacular journals more than two

thirds of the respondents (67.14%) had medium to high level of usage.

The journal Valarum Velanmai was mostly used by the respondents followed by Farmer'satisfied World. Kalai Kathir and Vignana Chuder. The journal Kalnadi Kathir was least used by the respondents.

3.3.4. Usage of Newspapers in the Library

Regarding usage of newspapers, 90% of the respondents had medium to high level of usage.

The newspaper Dinamalar was mostly used followed by The Hindu, New Indian Express and Dinamani. The newspapers Kathiravan and Dinaboomi were least used by the students.

3.4. Usage of Reference Books in the Library

As regards to reference books, most of the respondents (87.14%) had medium to high level of usage.

Regarding the usage of reference books, three characteristics viz., age, educational level of parents and annual income of parents were positively and significantly related at one percent level of probability.

The subject reference books, dictionaries and competitive exam books were mostly used by the students followed by year books and encyclopedias. The references books like almanacs and computer books were least used by the respondents.

3.5. Usage of Audio-visual Resources in the Library

Nearly four-fifths (80.72%) of the respondents used the audio-visual resources either occasionally or rarely.

Only two characteristics viz. age and educational level of parents were positively and significantly related at one percent level of probability with the usage of audio-visual resources in the library.

3.6. Usage of Digital Resources in the Library

More than two thirds of the respondents (68.57%) never utilized the digital resources in the library.

Two characteristics viz. age and annual income of parents were positively and significantly related at one percent level of probability with the usage of digital resources in the library.

3.7. Usage of on-line Resources in the Library

About 27.86 percent of the respondents did not know anything about Internet browsing and exactly one fourth of the respondents did not possess the skill in operating Internet.

About 29.29% of the respondents did not know anything about e-mail facilities and 40% of respondents did not having the skill in operating e-mail.

Two characteristics viz. age and annual income of the parents were positively and significantly related at one percent level of probability with the usage of on-line resources in the library and the variables community and sex were negatively and significantly related at one percent level of probability.

3.8. Usage of Reprographic Services in the Library

Just less than half of the respondents used the Xerox facilities frequently followed by 40.71% used the facilities occasionally.

Two characteristics viz. age and annual income of the parents were positively and significantly related at one percent level of probability with the usage of reprographic services in the library and the variable sex was negatively and significantly related at one percent level of probability.

4. Constraints in the Utilization of Library by the Students

The major constraints faced by the respondents in utilizing the library are as follows.

Four fifths of the respondents expressed that the availability of only a minimum number of International journals as constraint.

The study revealed that 69.29% of the students expressed that the number of library tickets supplied to them are minimum.

Just more than two thirds of the respondents (67.86%) reported the non-availability of latest issues of national journals.

Regarding Xerox facility, exactly half of the respondents reported that the Xerox charges were high when compared to local condition.

5. Suggestions for Effective Utilization of Library

The major suggestions given by the respondents for effective utilization of the library are as follows.

About 31.43% of the respondents reported that the evening time of library services should be extended.

Nearly one-fifth of the respondents (20.71%) reported that more number of chairs and tables should be increased in the library.

About one-fifth of the respondents (19.29%) told that more library tickets should be given to UG students.

About 16.43 percent expressed that the books should be given on lending even during Saturdays and the Xerox facilities should be extended on Saturdays.

About 12.86% of the respondents suggested the general improvement of library facilities.

6. Testing of Hypotheses

The hypotheses framed in this study were test verified and the results are given below.

H1 : There will be significant difference on the characteristics of male and female students.

Of seven characters selected for the study only community alone showed significant difference between male and female respondents and all the other variables did not show any difference among male and female respondents.

H2 : There will be difference in the time utilization behaviour of male and female students.

As regards to time utilization behaviour male and female student respondents did not show any significant difference.

H3 : There will be effective utilization of different components of library

The study revealed that the usage of text books, international journals, national journals and vernacular journals were low to medium.

The usage of reference books was medium and the usage of newspapers was high.

Majority of the respondents used reprographic services either frequently or occasionally.

As regards to audio-visual majority of the respondents used them either occasionally or rarely.

The study revealed that majority of the student respondents did not utilize the digital resources and on-line resources.

H4 : There will be relationship between characteristics variables and time utilization behaviour.

As regards to time utilization only two characteristics namely, age and medium of instruction at school were positively and significantly related at one percent level of probability which the remaining five variables namely, sex, rural/urban background, educational level of parents, annual income of parents and community were non-significant their relationship.

H5 : There will be relationship between characteristics variables and usage of different components of library.

Of the seven variables selected for the study only one characteristics namely age was positively and significantly relate at one percent level of probability with the usage of different components of library. The variable community was negatively and significantly related at one percent level of probability with the usage of different components of library, while the remaining five variables were non-significant in their relationship.

CONCLUSION

Library is a storehouse of rich resource in the form of books, periodicals, gazetter, yearbooks, e-journals including other digital resources. Proper utilization of the available resources is required for the students pursuing professional education to get acquainted with the latest developments and findings around the world. Hence, a study on the utilization behaviour of the students of Undergraduate and Postgraduate is required to understand their reading habit, their needs and the difficulties, what they face in the process of retrieving materials for their professional career. Hence, the present investigation is attempted to study the time utilization behaviour as well as the usage of the various components of the library with the following specific objectives:

1. To study the profile of students of Agricultural College and Research Institute, Killikulam.
2. To assess the time utilization behaviour of the students.
3. To study the extent of usage of various components of library.

4. To identify the constraints in the utilization of library by the students.
5. To make suggestions for effective utilization of the library

The study was conducted at Agricultural College and Research nstitute, Killikulam, Thoothukudi District of Tamil Nadu. One Hundred B.Sc. (Agri) students comprising of 45 males and 55 females and forty M.Sc. (Ag) students comprising of 19 males and 21 females were contacted for the study purpose. Seven independent variables viz. age, sex, rural/urban background, medium of instruction at school, educational level of parents, annual income of parents, community and two dependent variables viz. time utilization behaviour and usage of different components of library were selected for the study. The data were collected using a well-structured pre-tested interview schedule and the collected data were analyzed by using appropriate statistical tools.

The salient findings of the study are presented below.

I. Profile of students

All the respondents were young aged about 71.42 percent of the students were studying in B.Sc. (Ag.) and 28.58% were studying M.Sc. (Ag.). A majority of 72.14% of students were having rural background and 27.86% were having urban background. Among the students hailed from urban area nearly three fourths were females and the remaining one fourth were males. Nearly four fifths (79.29%) of the respondents studied in Tamil medium and exactly one-fifth (20%) studied in English medium. As for as the Tamil Medium is concerned 48.65% of male respondents and 51.35% of female respondents were from tamil medium. As far as English medium is concerned more than two thirds (67.86%) of female respondents and less than one third of male respondents (32.14%) were from English medium. About 64.29% of the respondents parents were educated and 35.71% of the respondents parents were uneducated. As regards to male respondents, 54.69% of their parents were educated and 45.31% of the parents were uneducated. Whereas in the case of female students 72.37% of their parents were educated and 27.63% of their parents were uneducated. About three fourths (75.01%) of the respondents were having less than Rs. 50,000 as annual income. About three-fourths (74.29%) of the respondents belonged to either BC or SC/ST. Most of the students belonged to Hindu religion.

2. Time Utilization Behaviour of the Students

2.1. Frequency of Library Usage by Students

More than half of the respondents (55%) frequently visited the library followed by 41.42% of the respondents visited the library occasionally and 3.58% visited the library rarely.

There is difference in the frequency of library usage between UG and PG student. Most of the PG Students (92.50%) used the library frequently and majority of the UG students (55%) used the library occasionally followed by 40% used the library frequently and 5% used the library rarely.

2.2. Time Utilization at the Library

About 45% of the respondents spent 20-30 hours in a month at the library followed by 24.28% of the respondents spent about 10-20 hours in the library. About 22.14% of the respondents spent more than 30 hours in a month and 8.58% of the respondents spent only less than 10 hours in the library.

The time utilization of the UG and PG students were analyzed separately and it is found that 85% of the PG students spent more than 20 hours per month in the library. Similarly 60% of the UG students spent more than 20 hours per month in the library.

3. Extent of Usage of Various Components of Library

3.1. Overall Usage of Different Components of Library

A majority of 86.43% of the respondents used the different components of library from low to medium level only.

The relationship of characteristic with the usage of different components of library by the respondents showed that out of 7 characteristics, only one characteristic viz. age was positively and significantly related at one percent level of probability.

3.2. Usage of Textbooks in the Library

Nearly four fifths of the respondents (78.77%) used the text books available in the library at low to medium level. More than one fourth of the respondents used the text books frequently on the subjects like Agronomy (35.71%), Soil Science and Agricultural Chemistry (29.29%), Plant Pathology (29.29%). Entomology (27.86%), Plant Breeding and Genetics (27.14%).

More than one fourth of the students never used the books in the subject like Food Science (52.14%), Environmental Sciences (42.14%), Crop Physiology (32.86%), Biochemistry (27.86%), Animal Husbandry (26.43%) and Economics (25.71%).

The relationship of characteristic with the usage of textbooks in the library by the respondents showed that only one characteristic namely age was negatively and significantly related at one percent level of probability.

3.3. Usage of Periodicals in the Library

Most of the students (86.43%) had only low to medium level of usage. Only 13.57% had high level of usage. The relationship of characteristic with the usage of periodicals in the library by the respondents was worked out and is found that only one characteristic, viz. age was positively and significantly related at one percent level. The variable community was negatively and significantly related at one percent level of probability.

3.3.1. Usage of International Journals in the Library

Most of the respondents (87.88%) had low to medium level of usage regarding International Journals in the library. Out of 13 International journals nine journals were used frequently or occasionally by one-third of the respondents and the remaining four journals were never used by more than half of the respondents.

More than one third of the respondents used frequently or occasionally the journals like Rice Abstracts (57.85%), Field Crop Abstracts (49.29%), Plant Breeding Abstracts (45.72%), Soil Science and Plant Nutrition (41.43%), Biotechnology Advances (39.29%), Review of Agricultural Entomology (37.15%), Agri Biotech news and information (36.44%), Horticultural Abstracts (35%) and Review of Plant Pathology (35%).

More than half of the respondents never used the journals like Weed Abstracts (53.57%), Agricultural Economics (52.85%), Seed Abstracts (52.15%) and Seed Science and Technology (51.42%).

3.3.2. Usage of National Journals in the Library

The majority of the respondents (86.43%) had low to medium level of usage of national journals. Out of 47 national journals subscribed in the library, 15 journals were used frequently or occasionally by the students, two journals were occasionally or rarely used by more than 60 percent of respondents, 29 journals were never used by more than 40 percent of respondents.

3.3.3. Usage of Vernacular Journals in the Library

Regarding the usage of vernacular journals more than two thirds of the respondents (67.14%) had medium to high level of usage. Majority of students used either frequently or occasionally the journals like Valarum Velanmai (70.72%), Farmer's World (60%) and Kalai Kathir (57.86%).

3.3.4. Usage of Newspapers in the Library

Regarding usage of newspapers, 90% of the respondents had medium to high level of usage. The newspaper Dinamalar (88.57%), *The Hindu* (87.14%), *New Indian Express* (71.43%), *Dinamani* (74.29%), The newspapers *Kathiravan* and *Dinaboomi* were least used by the students.

3.3.5. Usage of Reference Books in the Library

As regards the reference books, most of the respondents (87.14%) had medium to high level of usage. More than two third of the respondents used either frequently or occasionally the reference books like subject Reference books (87.14%), Year Books (80.71%), Competitive exam books (80%) and Dictionaries (77.86%).

To study the relationship of characteristic with the usage of reference books in the library, correlation coefficient was worked out and is found that out of 7 characteristics, three characteristics namely age, educational level of parents and annual income of parents were positively and significantly related at one percent level of probability.

3.4. Usage of Audio-visual Resources in the Library

Nearly four-fifths (80.72%) of the respondents used the audio-visual resources either occasionally or rarely. The relationship of characteristics with the usage of audio-visual resources in the library was analyzed and found that only two characteristics viz. age and educational level of parents were positively and significantly related at one percent level of probability.

3.5. Usage of Digital Resources in the Library

More than two thirds of the respondents (68.57%) never utilized the digital resources in the library. Only 17.86% of the respondents utilized the facilities either frequently or occasionally. To study the relationship of characteristics with the usage of digital resources in the library by the respondents, correlation coefficient was worked out and is competitive exam books (80%) and Dictionaries (77.86%).

To study the relationship of characteristic with the usage of reference books in the library, correlation coefficient was worked out and is found that out of 7 characteristics, three characteristics namely age, educational level of parents and annual income of parents were positively and significantly related at one percent level of probability.

3.6. Usage of on-line Resources in the Library

3.6.1. Usage of Internet Facility in the Library

Just more than one-fourth of the respondents (27.86%) of the respondents did not know anything about Internet browsing and exactly one fourth of the respondents did not possess the skill in operating Internet. About 22.14 percent of the respondents rarely used the Internet facility followed by 17.15% and 7.85% used the Internet facility occasionally and regularly respectively.

3.6.2. Usage of e-mail Facility in the Library

About 29.29 percent of the respondents did not know anything about e-mail facilities and 40% of respondents did not having the skill in operating e-mail. Less than one percent of the respondents used the email facility regularly, ten percent used the facility occasionally and 25% used the facility rarely.

To study the relationship of characteristics with the usage of online resources in the library by the respondents, correlation coefficient was worked out and is found that two characteristics, viz. age and annual income of the parents were positively and significantly related at one percent level of probability. The variables community and sex were negatively and significantly related at one percent level of probability.

3.7. Usage of Reprographic Services in the Library

Just less than half of the respondents used the Xerox facilities frequently followed by 40.71% used the facilities occasionally. Majority of 89.06% of male respondents and 82.89% of female respondents utilized the Xerox facilities either frequently or occasionally.

To relationship of characteristics with the usage of reprographic services was analysed and found that two characteristics, viz. age and annual income of the parents were positively and significantly related at one percent level of probability with the usage of reprographic services in the library and the variable sex was negatively and significantly related at one percent level of probability.

4. Constraints in the Utilization of Library by the Students

Four-fifths of the respondents expressed that the availability of only a minimum number of International journals as constraint. The study revealed that 69.29% of the students expressed that the number of library tickets supplied to them are minimum. Just more than two-thirds of the respondents (67.86%) reported the non-availability of latest issues of national journals. Regarding Xerox facility, exactly half of the respondents reported that the Xerox charges were high when compared to local condition.

The other constraints faced by more than one tenth of the students were the physical condition of the furniture and other accessories were not comfortable (42.14%), lack of easy access to text books (32.14%), high charges for Internet browsing (29.29%), reading atmosphere was not good (18.57%), and the library fine charges were high (18.57%).

5. Suggestions for Effective Utilization of Library

About 31.43% of the respondents reported that the evening time of library services should be increased followed by 20.71% reported that more number of chairs and tables should be increased in the library. About one fifths of the respondents (19.29%) told that more library tickets should be given to UG students and 16.43% expressed that the books should be given on lending even during Saturdays and the Xerox facilities should be extended on Saturdays. About 12.86% of the respondents suggested the general improvement of library facilities. Less than ten percent of the respondents suggested that the opening of library on Sunday also (7.14%), purchase of more number of general study books (6.43%), providing pure drinking water facility (6.43%), purchase of more civil service books (6.43%), providing more number of Tamil books (5%), Animal husbandry books (2.14%), Story books (2.14%), purchase of additional newspapers and magazines (2.14%), allowing reference books for lending (2.14%), purchase of soil science books (0.71%) and making library hours as compulsory to students (0.71%).

References

Al-Harbi, *Internet use by Graduate Students in Communication Department of Florida State University and its Impact on the use of FSU Academic Libraries*, The Florida State University, 2002.

Alzamil, *Perception of Internet use as Academic Library Services Delivery Medium for web-based Courses*, The Florida State University, 2002.

Arunkumar, Publishing on CD-ROM : Indian Potential DESIDOC *Bullet in of Information Technology*, 1997, 17(5), 24-26.

Babakisi, T. Fidzani, *User Education in Academic Libraries : A Study of Trends and Developments* in Southern Africa, 61st IFLA General Conference Proceedings—August 20-25, 1995.

Balasubramanian, K. and Neelakandan, K.,User Education University and Research Centres, *University News*, July 29, 1991.

Berenson, *et. al. Research and report writing for Business and Economics*, Random House, New York, 1971.

Chan, Maintaining Professional Competence : *Impact of Organizational and Individual factors on the updating activities of public reference Librarian*, University of Toronto (Canada), 2002.

Chopra, H.S., Electronic Library in the New Millennium vision of Library and Information centre, Viva Books, New Delhi, 2000, pp. 190-94.

Chopra, H.S., Library Information Technology in Modern era, Common Wealth Publishers, 1999.

Clabo, *A study of the library use practice of high school students in three east Tennessee*, East Tennessee State University, 2002.

Devarajan, A., *Information Technologies in Libraries*, Ess Ess Publications, New Delhi.

Dinamani, 20th November 2001, p. 6. *Encyclopedia Britannica*, Vol. 13. p. 1031, 1965.

Esperansa, M., *Library and Information Science*, Concept Publishing Company, New Delhi, 1995.

Fleming, Hugh (ed.) User education in academic libraries, Library Association Publishing Limited, London, 1990.

Gupta, B.L., Library Service, Pointer Publishers, Jaipur, 1989.

Handbook of Library and Information Science 1997/Association of Indian Universities, New Delhi, 1997.

Hey, Evaluating GIGA : *Resource discovery agents for digital Libraries*, University of Southampton (United Kingdom), 2002.

Hyman, *et. al. Interviewing in Social Research*, University of Chicago Press, Chicago, 1975.

IASLIC, *Information Super Highway : Its impact on Library and Information Services in India*, XXI All India Conference of IASLIC, 1997.

Information Super Highway : Its impact on library and information services in India, XXI All India Conference, 26-29, December, Tamil Nadu Agricultural University, Coimbatore, 1997.

Iyer, V.C. *Networking and the future of Libraries*, Rajat Publications, Delhi.

John, J.R. *Educating the Library User*, R.R. Bowker Company, New York, 1974.

Joseph Gibaldi, *MLA Hand Book for writers of Research Papers*, ed. 4, affiliated East-West Press Pvt. Ltd., New Delhi, 1996.

Kawatra, P.S., *Textbook of Information Science,* A.P.H. Publishing Corporation, New Delhi, 2000.

Khana, J.K. *Library and Society,* Haryana Research Publication, 1991.

Kim, *A Model of Digital Library Information seeking process (DLISP Model) as a frame for classifying usability problems,* Rutgers, the State University of New Jersey, New Bruniswick, 2002.

Kochhar, R.S. *Library Science : Today,* Discovery Publishing House, New Delhi, 1999.

Kothari, C.R. *Research Methodology : Methods and Techniques,* Wishwa Prakashan, New Delhi, 1985.

Majoo-Munshi and Karanjai, Documents supply service of INSDOC : A Selective Study of user Satisfaction, *ILA Bulletin,* 4. 1988. p. 188.

Majoo-Munshi, *Document supply service of INSDOC* : A Selective Study of user Satisfaction, *ILA Bulletin,* 4. 1988. p. 188.

Malavya, V.C. *Library Information Technology for the next millennium,* Manak Publication, New Delhi.

Malwad, N.W. *et. al.* ed., *Digital Libraries : Dynamic Store House of Digitized Information,* New Age International Limited, Bangalore, 1996.

Misra, R.P. *Research Methodology : A Handbook,* Concept Publishing Company, New Delhi, 1989.

Mittal, R.L. *Library Administration : Theory and Practice,* ed. 5, Metropolitan Book Co., New Delhi, 1980.

Mohamed Riaz, *Library Automation,* Atlantic Publishers and Distributors, New Delhi, 1992.

Murthy, S.S., Library and Information Services in the Electronic Information Era. *Journal of Library and Information Science,* 1999, Vol. 24 (1), P. 59 – 70.

Murthy, T.A.V. and Claubey, O.N., *Educating users about Library Catalogues in Library and Information Science,* Concept Publishing Co., New Delhi, 1997.

Mymoon, M. *et. al. Internet,* Ed by H.K. Kaul, Library and Information Networking, Naclin 2000, Delnet, Dec. 23-25, 2000.

Nageswara, Rao G., *Statistics for Agricultural Sciences,* Oxford and IBH, New Delhi, 1983.

Neena Singh, *CD Technology and Library : Excellence in Information Technology,* Raj Publishing, Jaipur, 2000.

Nowichi, *Students Success with World Wide Web Search Engines : Retrieving relevant results with respect to end-user relevance judgments,* Nova Southeastern University, 2002.

Nurdick, R.G. *Information System for Modern Management*, Prentice Hall of India, New Delhi, 1994.

Parameswaran, M., Collection Development in University Libraries : Policies and Procedures, *Desidoc Bulletin of Information Technology*, 1997. V. 17 (2), pp. 11-13.

Prakash Chander, *New Technologies and Developments in Library and Information Science*, Mangal Deep Publications, Jaipur, 1996.

Rajasekar, T.B. *Virtual Libraries : Internet-based Library and Information Services*, Paper in 17th Annual Convention and Conference of SIS held at University of Hyderabad during 12-14, March 1998. pp. 61-74.

Ravichandra, Rao I.K., *Library Automation*, ed. 2, New Age International Pvt. Ltd. New Delhi, 1996.

Rekha, T.P. *E-journals and its impact on Academic Libraries*, Proceedings of Caliber 2000, Chennai.

Riaz Mohamed, *Library Automation*, Atlantic Publishers and Distributors, New Delhi, 1972

Robbins, R., *Organizational Behaviour*, Prentice Hall of India, Delhi, 1989.

Samyasam, *Information Super Highway : A conceptual comparison with NII/GII and its impacts on society and the Indian Context*, Jawaharlal Nehru University Library, New Delhi, 1997.

Satyanarayana, N.R. ed : *User Education in Academic Libraries*, Ess Ess Publications, New Delhi, 1988.

Seetharam, S., Collection Development/Management in an Information Technology-based Environment : Current Initiatives and Issues, *Desidoc Bulletin of Information Technology*, 1997. V. 17(1), pp. 11-20.

Sen, J.P., *Virtual Library : A vision of the special library of the 21st Century*. Paper in XIX National Seminar of IASLIC held at MP Council of Science and Technology during 13-16 Nov. 2000. pp. 101-04.

Sethi, A.R., Library Co-operation in India, *ILA Bulletin*, Vol. 18 (3 & 4).

Sharma, R.K. and Tripathi, B.P., *Information Handling in libraries in 21st Century*, Ess Ess Publications, New Delhi.

Shukla, R.K., *Automation of Library and Information Science*, Concept Publishing Company, New Delhi, 1995.

Sridhar, M.S., *Managing Modernization of library science using IT in library and information science*, Vol. 2. Ed. By R.G. Prasher, Concept Publishing Co., New Delhi, 1997.

Srivastava, From Departmental Libraries to National Network, *ILA Bulletin*, Vol. 25 (4) January-March 1990, p. 157.

Subbiah, R., *Agricultural Librarianship in India : An Overview,* Metropolitan, New Delhi, 1988.

Thakur, R.S., *Information Super Highway and its Impact in Library and Information Services,* Technical Library and Documentation Centre, Calcutta, 1997.

The Hindu speaks on Libraries, Kasturi and Sons Ltd., Chennai, 2003.

Vasishth, C.P., *Modernization of Libraries,* Indian Library Association, Delhi, 1988.

Vijayakumar, P. and Sood, S.P., *Library and Information Science,* RBSA Publishers, Jaipur, 1991.

Woodword, H. and Mc Knight, C., *E-journals Issues of Access and Bibliographical Control,* Serial Review, Summer, 1995 : pp. 71-78.

XXI All India Library Conference of IASLIC, Tamil Nadu Agricultural University, Coimbatore, December 26-29, 1997.

Zeithmal, V.A., *et. al. Delivering Quality Service : Balancing Customer Perceptions and Expectations,* Collier Macmillan, London, 1990.

4

Use of Internet

INTRODUCTION

'Information' is the most vital resource for any kind of activity but it is difficult to define. According to Neuman and Neuman, "Information is that which destroys uncertainty". Today we are passing through a phase in which information is of key importance. It has been recognized as the fourth resource that has become one of the basic elements to determine the quality of life, the other three being men, material and money. Although, information has been the basic need of the society always but at no point of time, it has played such a crucial role as it is playing today. Inception of computer and communication technologies has brought revolutionary changes in the whole world of information, particularly during the last one decade.

Over these years, the life suddenly seems to have changed very fast. A tiny chip called the microprocessor began to take greater control of our lives. Organizations and institutions began to install computer for every small activity as if there was no tomorrow. Internet is gaining fast access in office culture as substantial numbers of information resources are available on Net. Perhaps, this is the most exciting period in the history of human race when world's most population is shifting from techno-illiterate to techno-literate. The society is undergoing a kind of transformation. With the passing of each day, we find that IT has affected almost every sector of our life, bringing a change the way people think, interact and do business today. It will not be surprising if in the near future the internet connectivity becomes a necessity of life just like connection to water tap, electricity and telephone lines.

Origin of Internet

The origin of the Internet can be traced back to 1969 with the beginning of the Advanced Research Project Agency (ARPA, later known as Defense Advanced Research Project Agency or DARPA, USA), sponsored by Pentagon just as a four node network. The objective of such a network then was to enable scientists in the Advanced Research Project Agency of US Dept. of Defense (DoD), to communicate among them. The four research laboratories connected on ARPANET grew by an average of one computer connected every twenty days. Later on other research and educational networks came into being and were referred to as the internet in 1977, the Transmission Control Protocol/Internet Protocol (TCP/IP), that underlay the Internet, were demonstrated for the first time. All the computers connected to the internet make use of common protocol, which is essentially a set of rules by which the communication takes place between the users on the network. In 1986, National Science Foundation (NSF) played a major role in the development of Internet with the creation of its network, NSFNet that acted as a backbone for growing network and connected 17000 regional networks. The regional networks, in turn, are connected to local networks, mostly supporting Universities to feed into this backbone. Now it is global collection of network of networks, the world's largest networking permitting the passage to all kinds of information exchange may be available anywhere in the world, with full freedom. Data travels across ordinary telecommunication lines and it is very easy for individuals and organizations to connect to internet.

What is Internet?

The global network of networks called 'Internet' is an information super highway that allows information to flow to unimaginable distances at an incredible speed. It is a network of networks which at one level is a vast collection of large and small interconnected computer networks, extending all around the world. At another level, it is all the people whose active participation makes the Internet a valuable information source. Abernathey defined Internet as a "Network of all kinds of computers that use myriad operating systems. Packets of data travel from system to system along the Internet, until they reach their destination. Internet's designers needed a linguafrance, the systems could understand, so the packets could go where they were supposed to go, event if some links in the Net were down. It is a loose network of millions of computers at thousands of sites around the world communicating to each other through a common language, the Internet Protocol. It is described as a loose network as there is no central authority to control the network".

Growth of Internet

Presently, Internet is growing at a very fast rate, spreading its roots at an unimaginable speed and becoming an integral part of our lives. No one had ever imagined that Internet would become so integral to the world when it started as a simple communication tool for defence personnel in sixties. It was just pain text, text and text. Today, there are moving pictures, graphics and sound that one never imagined off. All these developments have revolutionized the presentation of the information on the Net. There are over 140 million Internet users in the world hooked to over a 12 million host computers connected to the Net, and this number is growing everyday.

During 1990, the Internet was supporting commercial activities and the network was growing fast to include more and more sites. By the end of 1994, over 3.5 million hosts were connected and over 9.4 million by January 1997. Growth of Internet in India has been slow as compared to Western Europe and South East Asia. However, it has been assumed that the Internet access in India will grow at the rate of 164% in the next few years as completed to global growth rate of 59%. The traffic on the Internet is doubling every hundred days. The Internet has undergone, a virtual explosion, due to the enormous popularity of World Web. At present, more than 4000 Indian users have access to Internet through VSNL, and 7000 users from education and research community through ERNET. It accounts to a very small fraction of total population of India. Dept. of Telecommunication (DoT) and VSNL are the two key public sector bodies controlling internet till date, VSNL has presence only in 16 cities all over India.

Internet Service Providers and Popular Networks in India

Internet Service Provider (ISP) is the bridge between Internet and the customers with a point of presence on their network. The customers should have connection to one of ISP's server either through dial-up or lease-line. Until early 1990's Internet access was possible through some kind of dedicated line connection. Later with the introduction of various Internet access providers, dial-up accounts became available. By early 1994, more than hundred dial-up commercial Internet access providers were offering services in North America alone. Now there are various ways to get Internet connectivity, ranging from dial-up facility to satellite links.

According to NASSCOM, during early 1998, there were around 2,00,000 subscribers in India which would grow 1.5 million by the year 2000 and further to 8 million by 2002. In India, Videsh Sanchar Nigam Ltd. (VSNL) started the Internet service on 15th August 1995, till that time it was the only ISP.

Take off number at that time was only 4151, as the potentiality of this great facility was not realized by most of the people. But today, the scenario has changed, its subscription has grown to 2,50,000. Incidentally the growth rate has been very fast during the last decade. Today, there are 32 ISP in the country at different stages of their developments, well known among them are MTNL, ERNET, NICNET, Satyam Online, Bharti British Telecom, Mantra, Surevin, Dishnet and Siticable. The last two are operated through the cable network. Mantra is the latest ISP added on this list. Its popularity has increased manifold in India.

Though, India has been a late starter but off late, there has been much awareness about the role of internet and its potentialities. Today's information networks have broken down all the barriers of time and space enhancing users expectations continuously and creating the demands for more and more sophisticated, high quality information products and services. Today in India there are various networks offering online services through Internet. Some of them are as follows :

Educational and Research Network (ERNET)

In November 1986, Ernet was started by Dept. of Electronic (DoE) with the financial support of Govt. of India and a United Nations Development Program (UNDP) involving eight premier institutions as participating agencies, namely, National Centre for Software Technologies, (NCST), Indian Institute of Science (IISC), Bangalore, five Indian Institutes of Technology (at Bombay, Delhi, Kanpur, Khoraqpur and Chennai) and Dept. of Electronics (DoE), Delhi. Since 1989, it started providing Internet service to academic and research institutions in India.

The network started with few leading institutions and R & D organizations, etc. It has been quite successful in creating an awareness of Internet use among academic and research community in the country. Recently, it has been registered as a society under a new name ERNET India, under DoE. This network helps in conducting the research in various related areas involving major institutions in the country.

Softnet

The Dept. of Electronics, Software Technology Park of India (STPI) launched SOFTNET in 1993, which has started offering Internet service in collaboration with Setcom Service, India for software development companies. STPI has six centers located at Bhubaneswar, Trivandrum, Hyderabad, Gandhi Nagar, Noida and Bangalore.

NICNET

The National Informatics Centre Network (NICNET) is operational since 1987. NICNET covers all district head quarters, states/UT capitals and national capitals. Internet connectivity through NICNET has been made available via VSNL since 1995. It provides services to government organizations in the country by using satellite-based data communication of National Informatics Centre (NIC). NICNET has been offering Internet connectivity through dial-up mode under the service name RENNIC (Research and Education Network) to academic and research organizations. It is estimated that more than one million users (8000 institutions) are using NICNET facility in India.

Satyam Online

Satyam Online was launched in December 1998 as a first private internet Service Provider to announce the Internet service in 12 major cities in India. It proposes to cover more than 40 cities.

Mahanagar Telephone Nigam Ltd. (MTNL)

MTNL was launched in March 1999 in Mumbai and Delhi to provide Internet Service to general public.

Internet Connectivity Tool

Internet has made all the information resources available through connectivity tools. These connectivity tools, described in brief, as follows :

Electronic Mail (E-Mail)

E-mail, meant for exchange of electronic information, is the most popular feature of the Net. It is cost-effective and fastest mode of communication wherein one can correspond electronically with anyone, anywhere in the world. Mail is passed from one machine to another to reach its destination. For this purpose, person on receiving end must have an e-mail account. Messages can be sent or received in the form of text, graphics, images, photos and sounds.

File Transfer Protocol (FTP)

The Internet programme FTP is used to transfer of files from one computer to another, regardless of the file storage format or operating system. Through FTP one can copy files available on Net from anywhere. FTP requires specific address to the remote machine from where the file has to be retrieved.

Telnet

Telnet is the interactive facility, which allows one to access distant (remote) computer and use the information available on it, sitting on your own computer connected to Net. Once you are connected to another system, the same keyboard will become the keyboard of the remote computer and you can use their resources or download the information available on the other side. It allows access to library OPACs, commercial / bibliographic databases, remote CD-ROM databases and services provided by library networks like accessing union catalogue, etc.

Usenet

Also, referred as Bulletin Board System (BBS), is an electronic, message system for reading and posting messages. BBS is usually comprised of thousands of small groups of users, having common interest. It provides an opportunity to send and see the messages of one's interest. One needs a software 'News Reader' to retrieve only one news group news from a local Use net storage site and display it on one's own computer. Usenet groups are arranged in topical hierarchies like computer science, social, rec, news, talk, misc, etc.

World Wide Web

Also known as WWW, Web, W3 is the most powerful navigation tool on the Internet. It is based on a concept and technique called 'hypertex'. Words in one document are linked to another document. From the home page on web, one can go from one item of interest to another by selecting hyperlinks in the documents. Web provides access to information in the form of text, graphics, pictures and even sound.

The major features of the Web are :

- It is hypertext system
- It is a multimedia system
- It incorporates other internet tools such as FTP, telnet, gopher and wais, etc.
- It is a distributed system; and it provides an interface to other database systems

The most important concepts required to understand the underlying mechanisms of the web are client server architecture, the hyper text transfer protocol (HTTP), Hyper Text Markup Language (HTML) and Uniform Resource Locators (URLs) and others.

Gopher

Gopher is a menu-based programme to browse the resources of the internet without having any idea of its location. Gopher server accepts simple query and provides the clients a list of documents.

Veronica

Veronica stands for very common rodent-oriented netwide index to computerized archives. It is a programme accessible through Gopher. It allows quick access to information of Gopher to reach particular files and directories.

WAIS (Wide Area Information System)

Wais is full-text indexing software, used to index large text files, documents and periodicals.

Archie

It is a directory service available for searching the address of FTP servers around the world and one can Telnet to the Archie server.

REVIEW OF LITERATURE

Literature Review

This part is concerned with the review of literature directly related to the present study. It is in two parts viz. review of foreign literature and review of Indian literature. A review of the literature reveals that the teachers and the students are the most frequent users of Internet. They use Internet for teaching, learning and for research purposes.

Review of Foreign Literature

Becker (1998) conducted a study on the Internet use by 2250 teachers from public and private schools in the U.S. The study revealed that 90% of the teachers had Internet access. More than half of the teachers (59%) had Internet access at home.. A majority of the teachers (68%) a used Internet to find information resources for preparing their lessons.

Singh (1998) conducted a research study on the use of internet by the librarians in Malaysia. The main findings of the study indicated that 90% of the respondents used the Internet for work-related purposes. Most of the respondents were recent users.

Voorbij (1999) examined the use of the Internet amongst students and academicians in the Netherlands. A questionnaire was distributed among 1000 members of the academic community and three focus-group interviews were also held with faculty members. The study revealed that the web was being used primarily to search general, factual, ephemeral or very specific information. The study also revealed that students and academicians faced many problems while searching the web.

Williams (1999) reported the use of information technology and the internet in his project entitled "Information Technology in Michigan : Adult and Teen Survey Report". The results indicated that the majority of the respondents (72%) used the Internet atleast once a week and 45% atleast once a day.

Laite (2000) surveyed 406 graduate and undergraduate students from Shippensburg University. The survey showed that 57.6% of the undergraduate students used the internet 1-2 times per week and another 37.1% used it 1-2 times daily. More than 50% of the graduate students used Internet 1-2 times per week and 37.7% used it 1-2 times daily. The survey showed that the most used Internet service was e-mail. A hundred percent of the graduates and undergraduate students used e-mail services.

Nicholas *et. al.* (2003) conducted a study in the UK to examine the use to the web for health information and advice. More than 1300 people were surveyed. The study showed that 66% of the respondents accessed the internet from home, 28% from work place and the remainder (6%) used a combination of both work place and home.

Hanauer *et. al.* (2004) surveyed a diverse community college to assess the use of the internet by the students for health related information. The survey showed that although all the students surveyed had free Internet access through their community college, yet only 97% of the students reported having access to the Internet. The survey showed that 83% of the Internet users had access to the Internet at their home and 51% of the respondents accessed Internet at college or library. Eighty one percent of the students reported to access the Internet most for the college work and 80% for email/chat. Men and women searched for health information in almost equal numbers.

Asemi (2005) shows that all the respondents were using the Internet frequently because all faculties were provided connection to the Internet. It was revealed that the researchers of the University were getting quality information through the Internet. Fifty-five percent of the respondents searched for scientific information through the Internet because the University library had provided access to various databases and online journals for all the students and staff.

Bavakutty and Salih (1999) conducted a study at Calicut University, which showed that students, research scholars and teachers used the Internet for the purpose of study, research and teaching respectively. The purposes of internet use were : sending and receiving e-mails in connection with academic requirements, making a search on library catalogues, downloading images and communication with the peer.

Kooganurmath and Jange (1999) conducted a study, which revealed that a majority of the users used the internet for communication, followed by the access to information. More than 70% of the users used it for higher studies and only

39% used it for discussions with peer groups. The most used services of Internet were email, the web, discussion forums, FTP and Telnet.

A study conducted by Mahajan and Patil (1999) revealed that the purpose of using Internet by research workers at Pune University was to conduct literature search for students was to know curriculum based information for : teachers to find supporting information to write articles.

Naushad Ali (2000) conducted a study at Aligarh Muslim University, Aligarh. The study showed that more than 50% of the study population was satisfied regarding the timings of the Internet service, but were not satisfied with staff's cooperation, and reservation facility. Majority of the respondents were not happy with the number of nodes available.

Chandran (2000) conducted a study at Sri Venkateswara University, Tirupathi, which showed that more than 25% of the respondents used the internet for 2-3 times a week and more than 56% used it for accessing information. A majority of the respondents used the web and email services of internet. The purposes of using Internet included communication and information gathering. The sources used for identifying information about internet included website itself, journals and magazines, staff and newspapers. A majority of the respondents used general websites as compared to recreational and discipline-oriented websites.

Amritpal Karu (2000) conducted a survey regarding the use of Internet facility at the Guru Nanak Dev University, Amritsar. The study indicated that all respondents used interest for sending e-mail and 82% for web. More than 60% of the respondents used internet for primary information. 38% for secondary and only 15% used it for consulting OPACs. A majority of the respondents, i.e. 75.6% faced the problem of slow internet connectivity. All respondents used search engines to browse the required information. More than one-third of the respondents typed the web address directly and only 1.5% used subscription databases. The results of the study further showed that more than 80% of the respondents felt that in comparison to traditional documents, internet was time saving, easy to use, more informative, more useful and more preferred.

Kanaujia and Satyanaraya (2003) conducted a study of the Science and Technology Community of Lucknow city to assess the level of awareness and demand of web-based learning environment among Science and Technology information seekers. The major findings of the study revealed that 49.2% users browsed the Web for more than 2 to 4 hours and 14% for more than 5 hours a day. The study further showed that 36.6% users consulted e-journals regularly on the internet, 40.4% used internet for consulting technical reports, 24.8% to find online databases and 10.4% for telnet service.

Mishra, Yadav and Bisht (2006) conducted a study to know internet utilization pattern of the undergraduate students of G.B. Pant University of Agriculture and Technology, Pantnagar. The findings of the study indicated that a majority of the students (85.7%) used the Internet. Out of the internet users 67.7% were male students and 32.3% female students. The findings of the study also showed that 61.5% of the males and 51.6% of the female used internet for preparing assignments. A majority of the respondents, i.e. 83.1% male and 61.3% female respondents indicated that they faced the problem of slow functioning of internet connection.

RESEARCH DESIGN

Objectives

In order to persue this study following objectives are framed, in according with the scope of this investigation:

- ❑ To know the characteristics of the the population studied.
- ❑ To study the length and frequency of using internet by the respondents.

- To analyse the purpose and its frequency of internet using by the respondents.
- To study the frequency of use of internet resources and tools by the respondents.
- To know how the internet-based resources are identified by the respondents.
- To rank the features of internet resources by the respondents.
- To study the use of search engine and websites by the respondents.
- To know the extent of difficulties in accessing internet by the respondents.
- To know the reason for not using the internet service.

Methodology

This study attempts to examine the characteristics and internet using behaviour of the respondents studying in the IJCE Tuticorin.

ANALYSIS

Data Collection

The researcher has employed a well structured questionnaire for collecting the data from the students of IJCE.

The data was collected by using empirical methods of questionnaire. The well-tested questionnaire was distributed personally to the student community of IJCE. Sufficient time was given to the respondents in furnishing the information. 200 questionnaires were distributed to the respondents, out of which 195 were received back, making the response rate at 97.5%.

Statistical Techniques

The collected data were classified and tabulated according to the objectives of the study, and analysed by using statistical tools, such as percentage analysis and ranking analysis.

TABLE 1
Different Types of Websites Used by Respondents

Websites	*Number*	*Percentage*
General	131	87.91
Recreational	58	38.93
Discipline-oriented	42	28.19

Source : Primary Data.

Table 1 shows the different types of websites used by the respondents.

Nearly 90 percent of the respondents used general websites and 38.93 percent and 28.19 percent of the respondents using recreational and discipline-oriented websites respectively.

FIG. 1

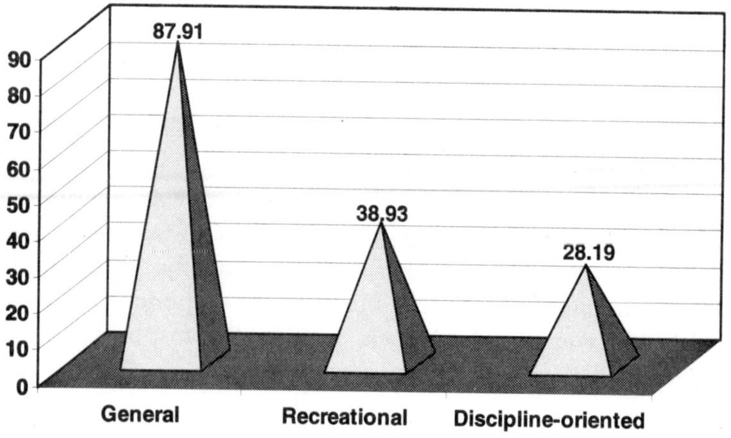

Discipline-oriented Websites Used by Respondents

Among the respondents 42 who have been using discipline oriented websites 92.86 percent of them using Engineering institution websites, 88.10 percent professional societies association, 85.71 percent colleges and universities, 76.19 percent companies, 73.81 percent mailing lists websites.

It is also evident from the Table 2, that only 26.19 percent of the respondents using full text publication websites.

TABLE 2
Discipline-oriented Websites Used by Respondents

	Nos.	%
Professional/Societies/Association	37	88.10
Colleges and Universities	36	85.71
Engineering Institutions	39	92.86
Companies	32	76.19
Databases	22	52.38
Publishers Home Pages	13	30.95
Newsgroup	21	50.00
Electronic Journals	18	42.86
Full text publication	11	26.19
Reference Sources	22	52.38
Mailing Lists	31	73.81

Reasons for not Using Internet

Table 3 shows the reasons for not using internet and its services. Among the respondents who were not using internet, twenty-seven did not now how to use it, twenty-one fear and anxiety, lack of awareness, don't feel it necessary, lack of time, and not getting what is needed.

0
10
20
30
40
50
60
70
80
90
100
88.1
Professional/Societies/Association
85.71
Colleges and Universities
92.86
Engineering Institutions
76.19
Companies
52.38
Databases
30.95
Publishers Home Pages
50
Newsgroup
42.86
Electronic Journals
26.19
Full text publication
52.38
Reference Sources
73.81
Mailing Lists

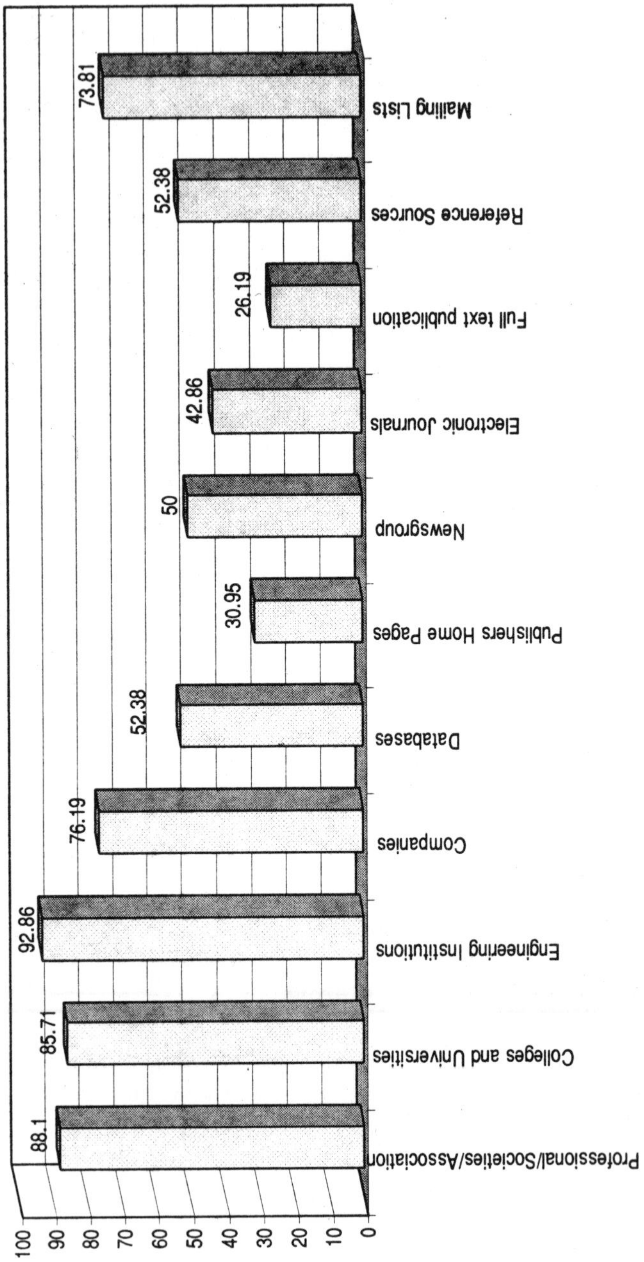

FIG. 2

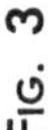
70
60
50
40
30
20
10
0
45
67.5
52.5
47.5
42.5
40
50
Don't feel it necessary
Don't know, how to use
Lack of facility
Lack of awareness
Lack of time
Not getting what is needed
Fear anxiety

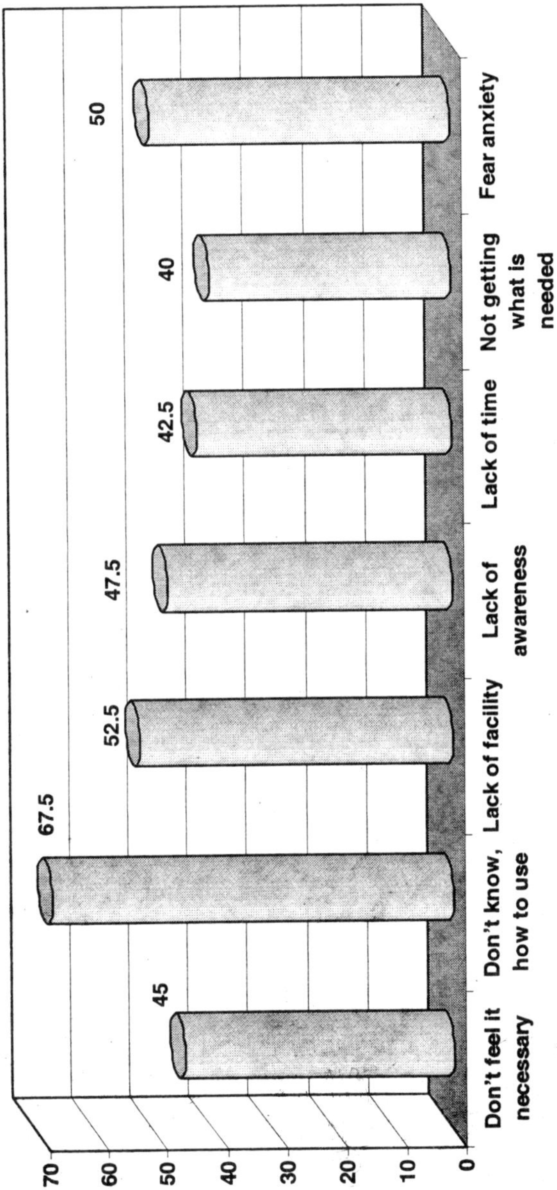

FIG. 3

Table 3
Reasons for not Using Internet

Reasons	*Number*	*Percentage*
Don't feel it necessary	18	45.00
Don't know, how to use	27	67.50
Lack of facility	21	52.50
Lack of awareness	19	47.50
Lack of time	17	42.50
Not getting what is needed	16	40.00
Fear anxiety	20	50.00

FINDINGS AND SUGGESTIONS

The following findings are arrived from the study. They are summarized and presented here :

1. The result found that most of the respondents are males.
2. Further the result found that majority of the respondents belong to day scholar students.
3. The result also found that majority of the respondents come from urban areas.
4. The result also shows that most of the respondents belong to backward class (BC) group.
5. The result also shows that 98 percent of the respondents have computer knowledge.
6. The result identified that 80 percent of the respondents made use of the internet.
7. The result shows that more number of respondents were accessing internet in cyber café.
8. The result of frequency using internet shows that 33.33 percent of the respondents are daily users of internet.

9. The finding of purpose of using internet shows that majority of the respondents using internet for the purpose of sending and receiving e-mail.
10. The finding of frequency of using internet resources and tools shows that world wide web (WWW) are the most used internet-tools by the respondents.
11. The result found that most of the respondents identified the internet based resources through personal communication.
12. Most of the respondents expressed as usefulness, accuracy and case to use are the major feature of the internet resources.
13. The result of the level of satisfaction with regard to use of internet in the college shows that majority of the respondents satisfied with staff incharge in the college internet service.
14. Most of the respondents using the yahoo search engine and 90 percent of the respondents using general websites.
15. The findings of extent of difficulty in accessing internet shows that slow accessibility searching, browsing, downloading are the major difficulties faced by the products.
16. Most of the respondents demanded course materials, websites, information and electronic document delivery services from the library.
17. Don't know and how to use it was the major reason for non-using the internet and its services by the respondents.

Suggestions

1. The use of internet at college is being made use of by a very few students. May be the factors like absence of well trained staff, time allotment, number of nodes available, and facility of printing,

have affected the use of internet at college. This usage needs to be increased.

2. Today, internet has become one of the important source of information and effective communication and retrieval tool, in libraries. Therefore the engineering college libraries should take steps to promote the use of internet.
3. The students in particular and everyone who is using in general have never realized the internet's potential in supporting library services and that internet facility should be extend to the library.

References

Asemi, A. (2005). Information Searching Habits of Internet Users : A Case Study on the Medical Sciences University of Isfahan, Iran. Webology, 2(1). Retrieved August 9, 2005, from http://www.webology.ir/2005/v2nl/a10.html

Bavakutty, M. and Salih Muhamed, T.K. (1999). Internet Services in Calicut University. National Convention Academic Libraries in the Internet Era. Organized by INFLIBNET, 18-20 February 1999, Ahmedabad, pp. 37-44.

Backer, H.J. (1998). Internet use by Teachers. Retrieved June 26, 2004, from http://www.crito.uci.edu/TLC/findings/Int -use/startpage.html

Butler (Mark). How to use the Internet; Join the Internet Revolution Today. 1994. Emeryvelle, Ziff-Davis press.

Chandran, D. (2000). Use of Internet Resources and Services in S.V. University, Tirupathi Environment. Conference on Information Services in a Networked Environment in India. Organized by INFLIBNET, 18-20 December 2000, Ahmedabad, pp. 3, 124-3. 127.

Chatterjee (Chinmay). Information Superhighway; papers of 21st All India Conference of IASLIC, 26-29 Dec. 1997. Tamilnadu Agricultural University, Coimbatore, p. 87.

Hanauer, D., Dibble, E., Fortin, J. and Col, N.F. (2004). Internet use among Community College Students : Implications in Designing Healthcare Inventions. *Journal of American College Healt*, 52 (5), 197-202.

Joe (Abrenathe). The Internet, PC World; January, 1995, pp. 132-39.

Kanaujia, S. and Satyanarayana, N.R. (2003). Status of Awareness and Demand of web-based Learning Environment among the S & T

Information Seekers. International Conference of Mapping Technology on Libraries and People, Organized by INFLIBNET, 13-15 February 2003, Ahmedabad, pp. 587-93.

Kaur, A. (2000). Internet facility at GNDU : A Survey. National Seminar on Academic Libraries in the Modern Era, Organized by IASLIC, 4-6 December 2000, Bhopal, pp. 199-24.

Kooganurmath, M.M. and Jange, S. (1999). Use of Internet by Social Science Research Scholars : A Study in Academic Libraries in the Internet Era. National Convention Academic Libraries in the Internet Era. Organized by INFLIBNET, 18-20 February 1999, Ahmedabad, pp. 478-83.

Laite, B. (2000). Internet Use Survey : Analysis. Retrieved May 21, 2004, from http://www.ship.edu!-bhl/survey.

Mahajan, S.G. and Patil, S.K. (1999). Internet : Its use in University Libraries in India. National Convention Academic Libraries in the Internet Era. Organized by INFLIBNET, 18-20 February 1999, Ahmedabad, pp. 483-88.

Mishra, O.P., Yadava, N. and Bisht, K. (2005). Internet Utilization Pattern of Undergraduate Students. *University News*, 43(13), pp. 8-12.

Narayanan (TN). Will India miss the Internet bus while the World Surf Ahead? *Electronics Today*; 30(5-6) 1998; 74.

Naushad, Ali, P.M. (2000). Internet and its use in Aligarh Muslim University : A survey Conference of Information Services in a Networked Environment in India. Organized by INFLIBNET, 18-20 December 2000, Ahmedabad, pp. 1.78-1.82.

Netizen Ram. *op. cit.*

Netizen Ram. *Rashtriya Sahara*, December 1999, 30.

Nicholas, D., Huntington, P., Gunter, B., Russel, C. and Withey, R. (2003). The British and their use of the web for health information and advice : A Survey. *Aslib Proceesings*, 55(5-6), 258-60.

Notess (Greg, R.) Gaining Access to Internet. *Online*; 16(15) 1992; 27-34.

Notess (Greg, R.). Internet Access Provides; *A Internet Resources*. Meckler, Westport, 1994.

Notess (Greg, R.). *op. cit.*, p. 238.

Notess (Greg, R.). The Internet Ency of lib & info sc., V. 49, 1997. Marcell and Dekker, New York, p. 237.

Raina (Roshan), Information Super Highway; Impact on Library and Information Services. Papers presented at 21st All India Conference of IASLIC, Tamilnadu Agriculture University, Coimbatore, 26-29 December 1997, pp. 91-92.

Singh, D. (1998). The Use of Internet among Malaysian Libraries. *Malaysian Journal of Library and Information Sciences*, 3(2), pp. 1-10.

Thambhekar (Ashok) and Pandian (S. Paul). Internet as an Opportunity for Libraries. In : Kumar (PSG) and Vashishth (CP), Ed. Caliber-99; Academic Libraries in Internet era. Paper presented at 6th National Convention for Automation of Libraries in Education and Research. Ahmedabad, 18-20 February 1999.

Vittal (N). Indian in the Age of the Internet. *Telematics India*; 10(9); 1998; 35.

Voorbij, H. (1999) Searching for Scientific Information on the Internet : A Dutch Academic User Survey. *Journal of the American Society for Information Science*, 50(7), 598-615.

Williams, J. (1999). Information Technology in Michigan : Adult and Teen Survey Report. Retrieved May 21, 2004, from http://www.pscinc.com/documents/cyberstate/finalreport.pdf.

5

Performance Evaluation

INTRODUCTION

Libraries in general, and academic libraries in particular around the world have undergone a radical change. The current librarians are facing new challenges and are assuming new roles. Walton and Edwards (1998) see this as an exciting time for LIS Staff. There has been a development of new competence in library workers at all levels, in order to respond to the vast technological changes, which are now taking place inside the academic campuses. All library and information managers are facing the challenge of improving quality and quantity of library services in the face of diminishing purchasing power. One method of facing the challenge is to have more efficient and productive staff members. In order to maintain and to improve efficiency and productivity of the library manpower, there should be a continuous process of performance evaluation of the staff in terms of various criteria keeping in view of strategic goals of the library and the organization. Majority of American Libraries employs a highly formalized system to evaluate the performance of each of their staff members (Johnson, 1972, p. 359).

Performance Evaluation

Performance evaluation is an on going process, which includes a clear definition of the employees' duties and responsibilities, the establishment of Performance standards, and a reasonable understanding of expectations and goals. It is a formal procedure to evaluate effective communication, with the aim to promote team effort in the unit and to determine Performance/merit level. The chief considerations of Performance evaluation are the level of Performance based on the job description and the achievement of annual goals.

Performance Evaluation of Academic Libraries

In recent years the operations of academic libraries have become increasingly complex as it involves mechanization, and computerization of library service. There has been a rapid growth in the size and scope of collections, in the variety of services offered, and also in the expectations of the users.

Performance evaluation concerns with a system evaluation which tends to determine whether a system has sufficient capacity to meet the demands that will be placed on it. System Performance is measured to understand how well the system is working and ideally how to improve the performance. With this aim of assessing the conditions of library services and recommending improvements that the present study is undertaken.

Evaluation is the assessment of goodness. It deals with the comparative study of the organizations' current Performance against some standard or set of expectations. Evaluation has two parts : the collection of information or evidence, about the organization or library's performance; and the comparison of this information with some set criteria. Different points of view needs different criteria, for example, for the purpose of the present study, priority has been placed on direct services to students, hence a criteria that focuses on students' needs is given more importance.

A library system can be accessed or evaluated in various ways of which cost-effectiveness is but one of the approaches to system evaluation, i.e. where both costs and their effectiveness can be assessed in monetary terms.

Performance then can be viewed from three perspective according to Mckee in his book planning library services.

(i) That of the resource provider; concerned with value in relation to costs.

(ii) That of the service provider concerned with quality as well as value.

(iii) That of the customer who will interpret quality of service in terms of a more or less satisfying experience when visiting the library and value in terms of the benefits gained from that visit. Some of these elements can be quantified and measured.

Measurement *vs.* Evaluation

Paul Evan Peters notes that performance measurement is a sub-specialty of performance evaluation. He emphasizes that there are things more in performance measurement, but on the other hand performance evaluation begins with measuring the things that can be measured, and adds that it is the quantitative expression of the desire for performance evaluation.

Measurement again involves the process of ascertaining the extent or quantity of something while evaluation refers to the process of determining it's worth or value. Worth can only be assessed from the user's point of view and somehow a method has to be found for measuring this.

Efficiency Analysis

Efficiency is nothing but the utilization of the most direct and simplest measures by which desired ends are attained, all unnecessary motions eliminated and waste of effort, time and material are avoided.

There is a gulf between the librarians' concept of the efficiency of his service and that of the users' concern. In this study stress has been laid on the need for libraries to consider user requirements and to shape their library provision to meet the changing needs of users.

Cost-effectiveness Analysis

Cost-effectiveness analysis is a method of comparing the costs of a library service with its impact on use. The prime purpose of cost-effectiveness analysis is to guide the allocation of resources in a library towards a maximum benefit.

Cost effectiveness analysis deals with the relationship between the cost incurred on the different units of the library and the levels of performance derived from them. It is a method used to assess the library system with a view to improve their cost-effectiveness, either by achieving the same objective at a lower cost or by achieving more objectives at the same cost.

Cost-Benefit Analysis

Another technique used for evaluating performance is cost-benefit analysis; its main purpose is to assist in decision-making. Such decisions might be about a library in its entirely, a function performed by the library, a service or product, an activity or even a resource. Costs and benefits should be described in terms of the unfavourable and favourable results of the comparison of alternative component, or service. However costs and benefits are not measured as direct outcomes or consequences, but rather in terms of comparisons of resources, services and so on. Comparison in this sense deals with the comparison of the service or system being evaluated with some alternatives.

Objectives of Performance Evaluation

The primary objectives of performance evaluation are to enhance the quality of library service and to promote the professional development of library staff members through a regular and systematic assessment of individual performance. A regular performance evaluation would make the employees positive about their job; motivate them to perform their best, grow and develop; make them to be benefited or genuinely helped; Appreciate them for their specific contribution; inform about future performance plans; and make them involve as a participant with the process.

The main objectives of performance evaluation can be summarized as follows:

- Work towards the attainment of the mission, goals and objectives of the library as well as the institutions.
- Inform the employees of their strengths, weaknesses and progress.
- Improve individual and team performance and productivity.
- Strengthen work relationships and improve communication.
- Develop employee skills.
- Recognize accomplishments and good work.
- Recommend employees for merit increases.
- Find out training needs of the employees.

Criteria for Performance Evaluation

Library and information professional will be judged on consistency of their job performance, grasp of library methods, command over their subjects, continued growth in their fields, judgements, leadership, originality, ability to work effectively with others and ability to accept their responsibilities to more general goals of the library and the institution (at http://staffweb.library.northwestern.edu/assembly/pesa.html) the criteria for evaluation of performance of library are divided into two broad categories, i.e. job performance and professional development and contributions. A list indicating some of the major areas where the librarians' job performance can be demonstrated below:

First Criterion

Job performance (statement of primary Responsibilities)—

(i) Acquisition, organization and preservation of library collections.

(ii) Assistance to users in their use of library resources.

(iii) Selection, building and management of appropriate collection.

(iv) Administration, coordination and supervision of library units, activities or systems.

(v) Application of judgement, analytical skills and appropriate subject knowledge.

(vi) Information delivery, information systems development and application.

(vii) Respected areas of competence or responsibility.

(viii) Seeks new challenges and provides creative ideas.

(ix) Adapts effectively to changing circumstances and requirements.

(x) Support of the curricular and scholarly endeavours of the faculty and students of the institution.

(xi) Makes effective use of the innovative techniques and tools.

(xii) Communicates effectively with faculty, students, colleagues and other insiders and outsiders of the library.

Second Criteria Professional Development and Contributions

In addition to performing their primary jobs, library and information professional are also expected to take active responsibility for the development of their own profession and of the continuing education. And to participate in appropriate professional and scholarly activities.

Professional Activity

(i) Attending at professionally relevant conferences;

(ii) Service to professional organizations at the local, state or national levels; and

(iii) Completion of professional continuing education programme or attending classes for academic courses or advanced degrees that are relevant to the librarian's areas of responsibility and workshops for the achievement of the appropriate professional competencies.

Scholarly Activity

(i) research, publication, presentations, production, design or exhibition of bibliographies, monographs, journals, articles, guides to literature, indexes;

(ii) research and scholarship using innovative information technology;

(iii) conference presentations as a speaker or on a panel;

(iv) teaching or directing educational programme of professional association or of other academic institutions;

(v) lectures for or of directing educational programmes of continuing education for librarians;

(vi) lectures in library schools, or other appropriate institutions of higher learning; and

(vii) taking active part in the development of the profession and professionals at local, state and national level.

Performance Rating

During a performance evaluation, numerous documents and comments from a variety of individuals that relate to performance may be collected and reviewed and summarized in order to make an assessment of performance of an individual employee. A performance rating summarizes and is delivered from evaluation process. It may take many forms: narrative numerical (e.g. a scale of 1 to 10), or categorical (e.g. outstanding, average, poor) as it show below.

Example of a Rating Scale

Grades	*Numerical* Rating	*Categorical Rating*
A	5	Distinguished performance (Outstanding performance) or Excellent
B	4	Noteworthy performance (Exceeding expectation) or Good
C	3	Full performance (Meeting expectation) or satisfactory
D	2	Diminished performance (below expectation) or Unsatisfactory
E	1	Unacceptable performance (unsatisfactory performance) or poor

REVIEW OF LITERATURE

Performance Measurements and Standards

A paper entitled Libraries of the Future was presented at 61st IFLA Council General Conference, Istanbul, Turkey. It describes the project undertaken by the IFLA section of University libraries and other general research libraries to develop guidelines for performance measurement in academic libraries using a number of specific criteria. The goals of the guideline are :

(i) To make it possible to obtain comparable result by applying the same indicators in the same way. This would help to solve the problem of lack of standards of indicators that measure performance.

(ii) To promote acceptance of performance measurement as an important tool for effective management.

In most organizations including the library, there is a formal control process based on some form of Management Information System (MIS). This is a planned system for gathering, processing and disseminating information so that effective management decisions can be made. Performance measurement measures actual performance against pre-set standards on targets, thus revealing any deviation.

The conference held in New Castle heard papers on performance measurement in academic libraries where Kikkoman and Koskiala emphasized the importance of combining evaluation process with the institutions and organizational process and also connect it with the organization's goals. They say it is a continuous process and should include user survey by pointing out the most important factor influencing quality that is user satisfaction. Different tools to survey users and their needs were described;

questionnaires, interviews and quality driven service agreements. Methods of performance measurement by measuring academic liaison or appraisal by staff members and managers were also used, but a major concern is the difficulty of measuring the unquantifiable. Experiments to apply benchmarking to the academic sector were also discussed by Kikkoman and Koskiala.

Having determined that library development in many countries should be significantly advanced through the availability of an international performance standard, McClure and others have give issues which include a consideration of the evaluation and development of library performance measures: the scope of the proposed standard; the content of and audience for a standard; the import of a standard on stakeholders; objectives and benefits of a standard; problems associated with development a standard; the potential for its implementation; and its impact on existing standard. An example of problems associated with development of standard is changing both in the user's need and in the technological field.

McClure *et. al.* have finally suggested a pre-standardization since not every country and type of library can implement either a basic or a more extensive set of performance measures.

Palmour *et al.* says that the development of planning process to be applied by individual library systems is rather to be preferred than provision of national or international standards. Through the planning process outlined here, libraries will set-up standards appropriate to the local continuous monitoring of progress.

In his book planning library services, McKee also hints that National or International standards may work in a context of uniformity and stability. However, in a context of diversity, with changing user needs and resource frameworks, a pattern of library determined objectives and regular planning cycles seem to be more relevant.

Achievements can only be defined in terms of intentions; this suggests that, in the context of library service, it is misleading to take only of performance measures. Assessing the benefit of a customer or user's gains from its library service is, the final analysis, a matter of informed value-judgment rather than measurement. However, difficulty arises in the use of student survey. Because satisfaction levels are determined by preconceptions and expectations, and responses are sometimes influenced by a desire to give the right answer, surveys can therefore produce results which are more subjective than objective. In order to obtain a more precise and objective response, measuring up points that questions about satisfaction in the user questionnaire should ask if they, the users, have found what they were seeking for in the library. Relevant questions live those concerning full rate should be included.

Morris Hamburg *et. al.* have also analysed the measures of library performance giving various advantages and disadvantages of these measures. For libraries, the active library aspect of promoting materials is important, document exposure measures are to be used. Morries *et. al.* affirms that library performance evaluation can be accomplished only by matching with the exposures accuring in any period of time the cost of facilities, equipments, and resources, etc. and contracted services are necessary to produce this exposure.

An essential part of any performance measures is a periodic matching of output (benefits) and input (costs) of an organization. Usually there is neither an attempt to measure library output nor to estimate the true costs of library operations as identified by Morries *et. al.*

Similarly in the Manual on the Evaluation of Information Centers and Services, they have described measures of individual performance of information center staff or library staff. The performance measures deal primarily with services to users involving specific or identifiable library user services, e.g., online database searching, inter-library borrowing, translation, etc., operational functions that involve a high degree of professional and intellectual work or production-like activities.

Griffith and King have listed functions and activities for which they have recommended maintaining measures of performance also presenting acceptable levels of performance. Suggestions related with the observing and controlling performance of staff have been provided. The use of tally checklists has been recommended which are used to record information on observation and defects. The tally of observations and defects at the end of a specified time would be compared to the acceptable number of defects appearing in the appropriate sampling guide. Any errors detected would require corrective action.

There is an immediate need for standardization of performance evaluation in assessment, so as to make easy comparisons between libraries. McDougall emphasizes on the same, he says the confusion surrounding performance assessment on evaluation is discussed in the context of inappropriately used and imprecise terminology, linguistic and cultural differences, lack of clarity over methods and implementation, false expectations and conflicting requirements of individualism and comparability and compatibility. He suggests manuals, standards, peer group work at local, national and international level and governmental agency support and assistance will promote clearer understanding and will suggest an optimistic future for the development of performance assessment.

Evaluation and Performance Indicators

The libraries need a framework that allows them to operate as managers, decision-makers, a proactive agents in control of their centers and for their innovative destiny, Evalyn H. Daniel in her book *Performance measures* examines the relationship of measurement with evaluation by saying there is no real purpose to measure performance unless some of the evaluation is utilized to bring out active changes. Evelyn has given three approaches to measurement, viz. the systems approach; the use of sampling techniques; and the need for greater statistical approach sophistication. Emphasis is laid on careful selection of appropriate tools to measure performance of the library by the librarian.

Mohr tackles the problem of system evaluation from two points of view :

(i) Use-oriented evaluation, and

(ii) Management-oriented evaluation. He says a problematic situation engenders an information need. This need is more or less well recognized by the user and expressed as an information request. And individual information service is then furnished by the staff with respect to the request. Mohr notes that the quality of the service thus delivered indicates the performance of the system.

A relevance to information request has been called management-oriented evaluation; Relevance to information need has been called as User-oriented evaluation. Mohr indicates that users will return to a service because of its effect upon work and because of the extended service to which their information needs are being satisfied. He further points out that for a genuine concern about the value and marketability of the information service, the judgment of the users has to be appreciated.

Employing the approach Orr presents a useful conception of how the various aspects of organizational performance are related to each other in libraries. Orr says the quality of resource and organizational effort are related somehow to the value of services delivered. Thus links among resources, quality, and value are neither direct nor obvious. He comments that libraries have always been required to demonstrate that they are operating at the lowest possible cost, or at a reasonable cost or at least honestly. The spending of the resources is the most measurable element according to Orr's model. It is much harder to measure the quality or value of what the library delivers. In part the lack of accenting for quality and value results from the difficulty of knowing what quality and value are in the context of library services.

There is need to mention the goal-based approach to assessment, which is the model, employed by accrediting agencies and professional library association standards. In goal-based assessment, the library asks itself if its goals address its mission and whether its programme and activities achieve these goals. A goal is the development in response to the question, what does the library want to accomplish? And it proceeds to an assessment of How well does it do it?

While this analysis by Patricia and Sara assess the degree of consistency between goals and performance, exploring the reasons for the results, and taking responsibility for the use of the findings.

In considering what to measure McKee too stresses that care must be taken on performance indicators used, an ill considered set of indicators can misdirect energies or pay attention to one area of the organization's work at the expense of the other. He gives three kinds of information which contribute to the evaluation of the library's current performance, viz. library statistics; responses on the citizen, user, staff and student survey; and measure of the library's achievements in relation to specific objectives or services.

Reviewing the basic principles, the role of performance indicators in quality assurance is to provide the quality target or standard of quality which is to be achieved. Library standards are shown to be neither objectives nor performance measures, they are either descriptive rules for proper management or qualitative rules for minimum input. While choosing performance indicators, the view points of the customer, manager, staff and funding authority have to be considered. Ian Winkworth in his work has identified that the primary quality of library is not the richness of stock as judged by many librarians but rather resource richness. He adds that if selecting performance indicators for individual activities is not easy then choosing a few summary indicators given two approaches to development search indicators : first approach rely on user satisfaction and second approach is to look at whether the library is delivering services to the standards set under individual activities.

Performance indicators can be derived from the goals of an academic library and practicable measures can then be explored for these indicators. The advantages and disadvantages of user survey in performance measurement should considered as this is the methodology chosen for several of the measures. Melanie has developed a precise survey method with a novel feature; a fairly concise survey form provided results both on which broad service areas most needed improvement and specific areas where improvements would be most useful.

Quality Assurance

Any quality assurance programme which does not have clear targets related to outputs or outcomes will have difficulty establishing whether or not it is successful. Away from quality assurance or control there is another factor as given by Hans Lofgren as critical success factor analysis. This analysis seeks to identify factors of particular importance to the success of individuals, departments, organizations, etc. The priority and performance evaluation methodology developed from the critical success factor approach, can be applied to identify areas of strength and shortcoming and to measure organizational success.

Document Exposure

The concept of document exposure includes two aspects:

(a) a passive aspect of satisfying demands by users for library materials and information; and

(b) an active of promoting library materials to create demands and to influence them. If a library creates demands that otherwise would not exist, document exposure increases, if a library improves its ability to react to and satisfy demands by users, document exposure tends to return for future exposure. Unsatisfied demand is lost and disappointed users often do not return.

Benchmarking

Benchmark is a fixed point of reference and is similar to the surveying concept. Benchmark law provides insight into the relative or absolute merits of different software packages in the library as well as hardware performance, i.e. how well a particular machine works. Once result of different approaches to performance measurement has been obtained, they must be utilized to build a decision-making system.

Benchmarking is a continuous learning and improvement process. It involves identifying the processes to be benchmarked, searching out superior employed in other organizations, recognizing the gap, and making changes to improve one's performance. Benchmarking is valuable because it helps an organization, understands its own performance and compares it with the best in its class.

RESEARCH DESIGN

For the successful conduct of any research study and meaningful inference, an appropriate methodology is indispensable. The main-focus of this study is to evaluate the performance of IJCE, Tuticorin.

Needs for the Study

This study is confined to evaluate the performance of IJCE. The main aim of the study is to evaluate the performance in terms of providing various services, facilities and collections of the library which will be helpful to moderate the present existing system in providing effective information service to its user community. It is also helpful in identifying where the level of performance should be increased.

Objectives of the Study

The following are the major objectives of the present study:

1. To find out the performance of borrowing facilities of the library.
2. To know the performance of library to fulfil users' requirement.
3. To identify the level of performance of library collection.
4. To find out the level of performance of information services of the library.
5. To measure the level of performance in reading material arrangement.
6. To find out the performance of infrastructure facilities of the library.
7. To know access to Evaluation-journal by the respondents.
8. To know the satisfaction with Evaluation-resources by the respondents.
9. Satisfaction with environment facilities to access internet.
10. To measure the level of performance regarding the use of internet in the college library.

Hypothesis

Based on the above mentioned objective the following hypothesis have been formulated and tested in the present study:

- There is a difference in the performance of borrowing facilities.
- There is a difference among the level performance of library collection.
- There is a difference among the performance of library service.
- There is a difference among the performance of environmental facility to access internet.
- There is a difference among the performance with regard to the use of internet in the college library.

Limitations of the Study

The study is restricted only to student users of Government Polytechnic College Library, Tuticorin. Other types of users such as faculty and research scholar were not taken as respondents for this study.

Methodology

The study is mainly based on the primary data collected from the college library users though a well-designed questionnaire. Also secondary data has been collected from sources like Text books, reference books, National and International Journals and Magazines.

Development of the Questionnaire and Collection of Data

The data was collected by using empirical method of questionnaire. At first, a pilot study was conducted to test the feeling among the respondents in answering the questions. Then the well tested questionnaire was distributed personally to the Library users. Sufficient time was given to the respondents for furnishing the information. At the time of collecting in the field questionnaire each respondent was requested to offer his comments and opinion on various concepts included in it. Their suggestions relating to the improvement of library services were also called for.

About 175 questionnaires were distributed to the users of library and 141 received back. The 41 respondents from aeronautical engineering, computer science engineering, electrical communication engineering, electrical and electronics engineering, mechanical engineering, information technology and business administration are taken for this study.

Statistical Techniques

To analyse the collected data, simple percentages and two-way analysis of variance were applied—

Chapter Scheme

- First Chapter gives an introduction about objectives of performance, academic library performance evaluation, criteria for performance evaluation and rating of performance.
- Second Chapter deals with review of literature to performance evaluation.
- Third Chapter examines research design which include objective, Hypothesis, methodology, application of statistical tools.
- Fourth Chapter give the profiles of Government Polytechnic and its library, Tuticorin.
- Fifth Chapter deals with the result and discussion of the related study.
- Sixth Chapter deals with findings and conclusion.

TABLE 1

Sex-wise Distribution of Respondents

Sl. No.	Sex	Aero	CSE	ECE	EEE	ME	IT	MBA	Total
1.	Male	12	11	10	12	18	10	13	86
2.	Female	8	10	9	8	—	10	10	55
	Total	20	21	19	20	18	20	23	141

Source : Primary Data.

Table 1 shows the sex-wise distribution of respondents.

Among the 141 respondents 59.57% are males and 39.00% are females. It is also evident from the table that the male students are more in number compared to female students. It is also found that in the Mechanical Engineering branch there is no female students.

FIG. 1

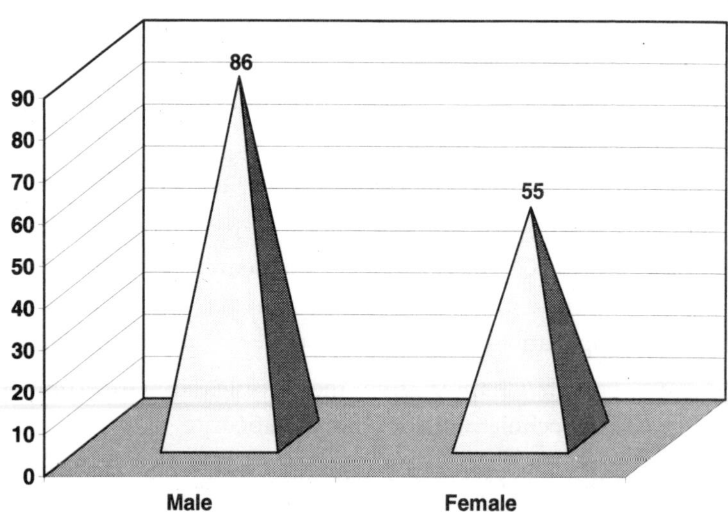

Table 2 shows the membership to learned societies/ associations by the respondents.

About 73.76% of the respondents has not registered as a

TABLE 2

Membership to Learned Societies/Associations

Sl. No.	Membership	Aero	CSE	ECE	EEE	ME	IT	MBA	Total
1	Yes	5	3	4	5	4	4	12	37
2	No	15	18	15	15	14	16	11	104
	Total	20	21	19	20	18	20	23	141

Source : Computed from Primary Data.

member to any learned societies or association whereas only 26.24% of the respondents has registered as a member in reputed associations.

It is also inferred from the table that the respondents from MBA department are more in number compared to other departments in getting the membership.

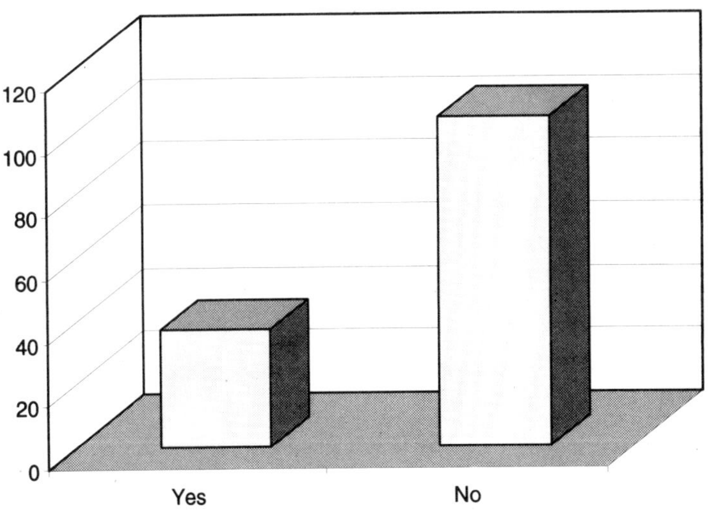

Table 3 shows the performance of library to fulfil user's requirements.

Among the respondents 63.12% of them has commended on the fulfilment of the user's requirements as excellent, 26.24% of them has said than it is adequate and no body says

TABLE 3
Performance of Library to Fulfils User's Requirement

Sl. No.	*Level of performance*	*Aero*	*CSE*	*ECE*	*EEE*	*ME*	*IT*	*MBA*	*Total*
1.	Excellent	12	13	12	13	12	13	14	89
2.	Adequate	6	5	5	5	5	5	6	37
3.	Fair	2	3	2	2	1	2	3	15
4.	Inadequate	0	0	0	0	0	0	0	0
5.	Poor	0	0	0	0	0	0	0	0
	Total	20	21	19	20	18	20	23	141

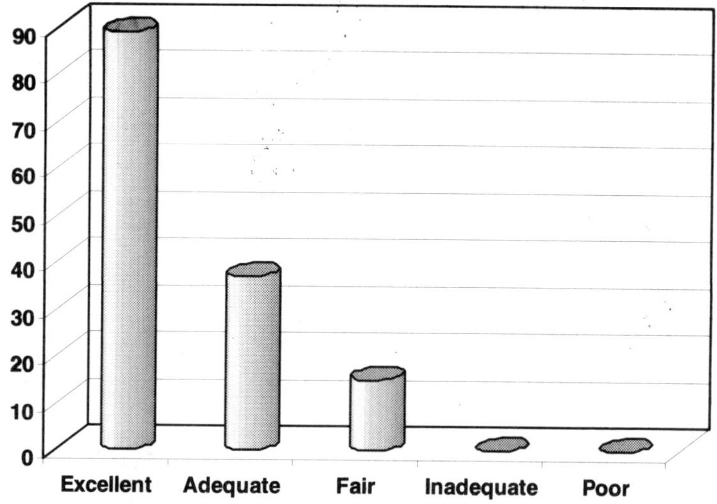

that the collections of the library inadequate and poor to fulfil their requirements.

FINDINGS AND SUGGESTIONS

Among the 141 respondents 20 (14.18%) from Aeronautical Engineering, 21(14.90%) from Computer Science Engineering, 19 (13.48%) from Electrical and Electronics

Engineering, 18 (12.76%) from Mechanical Engineering, 20 (14.18%) from Information Technology and 23 (16.31%) from Business Administration department are taken for this study.

Among the 141 respondents 59.57% are male and 39.00% are females. It is found that male students are more in number compared to female students. It is also found that in the Mechanical Engineering branch there is no female students.

It is found that majority of the respondents belongs to the age group of 22 to 25.

The result shows that the respondents from MBA department are more in number compared to other departments to register membership in association.

Among the 141 respondents 123 (87.23%) of them satisfied with borrowing facilities and the remaining of them are not satisfied. So, majority of the respondents satisfied with the borrowing facilities available in the library.

Among the respondents 63.12% expressed as excellent, 26.24% says adequate and no body says that the collections of the library are inadequate and poor to fulfil their requirements.

The result shows that the performance of collection of library is in very satisfactory level.

The level of performance of existing information service of the library shows that more than 80% of the respondents very much satisfied with the services and more than 90% of the respondents satisfied with reprographic service provided in the college library. In general, percent satisfaction is gained by the respondents from the library.

The library of performance of arrangement of reading material results shows that among the respondents more than 85% of them fully satisfied with the text book arrangements, journal arrangements, reference book arrangements and non-book material arrangements.

The performance of infrastructure, working time and procedure of the library shows that more than 95% of the respondents are satisfied and only a few of the respondents are not satisfied with them.

The performance of the library by providing facilities to access E-journal from the internet is in good.

The performance of the library by providing E-resources to its users shows that among the 137 respondents 125 (91.24%) respondents are satisfied with E-resources available in the library, only 12 (8.76%) are not satisfied with them. So it is evident from the statistical report that the library is providing satisfied E-resources service to its users.

The analytical report on the level of performance with environmental facilities to access internet in the library that among the respondents, 91.24% of them are very much satisfied and 7.30% of them satisfied with the environmental facilities in the library.

The research on the level of performance with regard to the user of internet in the college shows that more than 80% of the respondents are highly satisfied with regard to the use of internet in the college library except time allotment, it is nearly 75% and remaining of them are satisfied in this facility. It is also evident from the analysis that there is a single respondents who is not satisfied with the internet facilities.

References

Ann Sacks, Patricia and Lou Whildon and SARA. Preparing for Accreditation : A Handbook for Academic Librarians, Chicago : ALA, 1993.

Boekhorst, P.T., Measuring Quality : The IFLA Guidelines for Performance Measurement in Academic Libraries. *IFLA Journal*, 1995.

Daniel, Evelyn H. 'Performance Measures for School Libraries'. Advances in Librarianship, Vol. 6, New York, 1976.

Edwards, R.G. and Williams, C.J. Performance Appraisal in Academic Libraries : Minor Changes or Major Renovation, *Library Review*, 47(1), 1998, pp. 14-19.

Griffiths, Jose-Marie and King Donald W., A manual on the Evaluation of Information Centers and Services. New York, AGARD, 1991.

Hamburg Morris *et. al., op. cit.*, pp. 20-25.

Hamburg Morris *et. al.* Library Planning and Decision-making Systems. United States of America. The Colonian Press Inc., 1974.

Harris, Melanie, The User Survey in Performance Measurement. *British Journal of Academic Librarianship*, 1991.

Johnson, M. Performance Appraisal of Librarians : A Survey. *College and Research Libraries*, 33 (September 1972). pp. 359-67.

Kokkonen, O. and Koskiala, S. Performance Measurement in Academic Libraries. 1995.

Lan Winkworth. Performance Indicators.

Lofghan, Hans, Priority and Performance Evaluation : A Tool for Libraries. *Australians Library Journal*, 1992.

Mcclure, Charles, R. and other, Feasibility of an International Standard on Library Performance Measures. 1994.

McDougall, Allan, Performance Assessment : Today's Confusion, Tomorrow's Solution? *IFLA Journal*. 1991.

Mckee, Bob. *op. cit.*, p. 157.

Mckee, Bob. Planning Library Services. London, Clive Bingley, 1989.

Mohr, M. Systems evaluation in Terms of User Need. *Manuscript in New Trends in Documentation and Information*. Ed. by Peter J. Taylor. Aslib, 1980.

National, Consumer Council. *Measuring up : Assessment of Local Authority Services : A Guideline Study*. Quoted by Bob Mckee in Planning Library Services, 1986.

Ohio, Performance Review System. (Web Page : Accessible via internet at: http://www.state.oh.us/oprs.htm.

Orr, Richard, H. Measuring the Goodness of Library Services : A General Framework for Quantitative Measures', *Journal of Documentation*, 1973.

Palmour *et. al.*, A Planning Process for Public Libraries.

Performance Evaluation and Salary Administration for North Western Library Librarian. (Web Page : Accessible via internet at http://staffweb.library.northwestern edu/assembly/pesa.html.

Productivity News, Vol. 36, January-February, 1998.

Stone, Sue, *Library Surveys*. (2nd revised ed.) London, Clive Bingley, 1982.

Walton, G. and Edwards, C. The Impact of Evaluation-lib : The Emerging Paradoxes. *Library and Information Research News*, 21 (69). 1998. pp. 12-16.

Index